TRACEY EMIN

Tracey Emin is an artist whose work has been exhibited in galleries and collected by museums throughout the world. Although known as a visual artist, her confessional writings have always formed the backbone to her work. Until now, her only publications have been limited for collectors. *Strangeland* is the first full-length collection of her writing, which draws together new and some revised work from the past twenty-five years.

STRANGELAND
TRACEY EMIN

SCEPTRE

First published in Great Britain in 2005 by Hodder and Stoughton
A division of Hodder Headline

A version of 'Like a Hook from the Sky' was previously published as *Exploration of the Soul* (Tracey Emin, 1994; reprinted by Counter Editions, 2003). Excerpts from 'Like a Hook from the Sky' appeared in *Typical Girls* (Sceptre, 1997). 'The Proper Steps for Dealing with An Unwanted Pregnancy' appeared in *i-D* Magazine (Anniversary Issue, 2002). Excerpts from 'The Mummy Screams' were published in *The Times* (24 January 2001), and in *GQ* Magazine (July 2001).

'The Sun Has Got His Hat On' Words and Music by Ralph Butler and Noel Gay © 1932, West's Limited/EMI Music Publishing Limited (50%)/Richard Armitage Limited (50%). Reproduced by permission of West's, London WC2H 0QY and Music Sales Limited. All Rights Reserved. International Copyright Secured.

'Night Boat To Cairo' Words and Music by Michael Barson and Suggs © 1979 Reproduced by permission of EMI Music Publishing Ltd, London WC2H 0QY.

'Stuck In The Middle With You' Words and Music by Gerry Rafferty and Joe Egan © 1972, Icon Music Limited Universal Music Publishing Limited (50%)/Baby Bun Music Limited (50%). Used by permission of Music Sales Limited and Baby Bun Music Limited. All Rights Reserved. International Copyright Secured.

A Sceptre paperback

5

A CIP catalogue record for this title is
available from the British Library

ISBN 978 0 340 76946 1

Typeset in Baskerville by Palimpsest Book Production Limited,
Grangemouth, Stirlingshire

Printed and bound by Clays Ltd, St Ives plc

Hodder Headline's policy is to use papers that are natural, renewable and recyclable products and made from wood grown in sustainable forests. The logging and manufacturing processes are expected to conform to the environmental regulations of the country of origin.

Hodder and Stoughton Ltd
A division of Hodder Headline
338 Euston Road
London NW1 3BH

For my mum and dad with all my love
and thank you for making me so independent

I poured out my worries to a friend
Hoping it would make me feel better
But what I told him became an open secret
Fireflies in the dark.

Ahmad Ibu-al-Qaf,
eleventh century

MOTHERLAND

Like a Hook from the Sky

When I was born, they thought I was dead. Paul arrived first, ten minutes before me. When it was my turn, I just rolled out, small and yellow with eyes closed. I didn't cry. But at the moment of my birth into this world, I somehow felt a mistake had been made. I couldn't scream or cry or argue my case. I just lay motionless, wishing I could go back where I'd come from.

They put me into a little glass box and slowly I came round.

Paul and I would lie together in our cot. He would always be going on about something or other and no one could understand him, except me. But I would lie quietly on my back with my arms stretched out towards the sky, constantly pulling my hands through the air, holding on to the invisible lines that only I could see, the strands that join every moment: past, present and future. The lines that join every part of human destiny from eternity to the stars.

As a baby, I tried to die a couple of times. My most successful attempt was suffocation by pressing my mouth against the side of the carrycot. But Paul saved me – saved me with his constant screaming. It seemed that he would always be there, looking out for me. It was hard not to feel resentful. After all, my soul had been floating along when, somehow, it got caught up in his conception. It was like a hook in the sky – I was pulled down and turned into a creature of this world.

The first words I ever heard – the first that weren't Paul's – were 'The deaf and dumb are one year old, one year old today.'

I didn't talk until I was three. One day, my dad took me into the garden. He lifted me in his arms and pointed to a tree. And as he held me on that autumn chill morning, my first words sprang from my lips. 'Look. Apple.'

It was supposed to have been the last night our mum and dad spent together. This was 1962; Mum was married, Dad was married, but not to each other. My mum was twenty-one when she first gave birth – to my older brother, Alan – and she always said that you could not imagine the pain, that any woman who claimed it didn't hurt was lying. When she fell pregnant by my father, she booked into a clinic to have an abortion, only to talk herself out of it at the last moment.

This wild, roaming Turk, who had hit the London property scene and swept her off her feet, now came up with an offer: three days a week or nothing. Mum changed her name from Cashin to Emin and settled for three days a week, knowing he would never divorce his wife. Later, after his bankruptcy and a trail of financial disasters, she would be left with nothing.

But some things are meant to be for ever . . .

I sat by the tomato plants, Mum and Dad screaming at each other. I pulled a bamboo stick away from one. The weight of the tomatoes dragged the green stem down to the dirt. As they argued, I pushed the stick through the top of my thigh. Blood started to pour. And they stopped screaming.

Hotel International, that was where Paul and I grew up. A seventy-bedroom maze, along Margate sea-front, overlooking the Winter Gardens. It was actually six small guest-houses joined together, full of strangers, guests, kitchen staff and chambermaids, a juke-box and the Blue Room, where we used to dance. We were rich and spoilt and spoke three languages: English, Turkish and, of course, our own.

Because the hotel was six guest-houses, it had six back-yards, connected via holes smashed in each of the adjoining walls: a world of camps and bases, sheds and chalets, roofs and garages. A vast territory, a kingdom, our domain. We were rich – and envied. I remember hiding unwrapped

Christmas presents under the bed, just hoping they would disappear.

All Paul and I wanted was to be normal, like other children. But it was impossible. We were the twins. We had our own language until we were five years old. We shared a bedroom and sat next to each other at school. Once, we had shared a womb and now we shared a compulsive need for attention, which at times we liked and at others we hated.

Mum explained to us that they weren't sweets: they were pills, very special pills. And because of these special pills, Paul and I stayed special. If she took one every day, she would not have any more babies. We were six years old and tired of being special. We went to her handbag, removed the pills and, one by one, put them down the sink.

We didn't get a baby brother or sister. Instead we were given a rabbit. A tiny white ball of fluff. It had a little house. Paul made it a bed out of shoeboxes and I started on its clothes: a jacket, hat and tiny shoes made of serviettes. On warm summer days it would bounce round amid the wild strawberries and Paul and I would laugh, the joy of unconditional love.

As we got older, our world came to seem more and more unnatural – and we knew it. We first began to notice around the time our rabbit died. Of course, it had not simply died: it had been murdered, starved to death by the kitchen staff. We had been away in London. When we came home, the first thing we did was rush through the hotel into the yard and through the hole in the wall to what we called the green garden where our rabbit lived. The hutch was there, but no rabbit. The staff came out of the hotel in twos and threes calling, 'Rabbit, Rabbit.' They looked under pieces of wood, behind doors, under car wheels, in bushes, sheds and bins. Paul and I stared deep into each other's eyes: it didn't matter what anyone said, we knew they had killed it. The one real living thing that, individually, we had both chosen to love: gone. Our fluffy white rabbit.

Soon after Rabbit died Paul and I contracted whooping-cough. We lay next to each other in Mum's double bed, delirious, sweating, coughing our guts up. Even in our illness, we were desperate to get well and so bored – with the attention and fuss and gifts. One day I woke up and Paul was standing on a chair, naked, in the middle of the room, holding a catapult. As he pulled back on the elastic he said, 'I feel better.' Suddenly, I was screaming, my eye was burning. People ran into the room. *Wham* – he had flicked a lighted cigarette butt into my face where it had been caught neatly between the lids of my left eye.

The twins are well.

We were well, but we didn't go back to school. And we carried on sharing a double bed. We would scream and fight, pulling each other's hair, biting and scratching, demanding each other's space.

Paul and I walked round the square. A gang of other kids stood on the corner. They were all looking at a pile of dog shit.

'Go on, Emu,' one said. 'I dare you to walk through it.'

'Yeah, go on,' said the others.

I looked at Paul and said, 'Don't.'

Paul put out his hand and said to the others, 'Give us all your money.'

Then he walked straight through the shit.

As me and Paul walked home – him scraping his shoes – I said, 'Why, Paul? Why did you do it?'

He pulled a handful of money out of his pocket, shook it around in his hand and said, 'It's only shit, sis.'

I understood. I understood that Paul and I were different, and we would grow apart.

One day, I woke up to the sound of hundreds of bells ringing. The room was full of smoke and flames lapped round the bed like a giant ocean. Ismile, our mum's lover, was beating at them with his bare hands. I remember being carried away in his arms.

Paul stood in the hallway, smiling. He had set the bed alight. For a while we had our own rooms.

Then there were no rooms, no hotel, no guests. Dad was gone: he had lost his money and lost the hotel. As the Hotel International was being boarded up, my mum frantically carried our furniture across the yard to the cottage, the old staff house.

We didn't own the cottage, we just lived there. We had to: there was nowhere else to go. It was a comedown but we didn't care: we felt we were normal, living in this tiny house with our mum.

And we were wild and free. We spent the summers swimming, listening to Buddy Holly and the Beach Boys, wearing star-spangled plimsolls, watching the *Banana Splits* and covering our bedroom walls, from ceiling to floor, with posters. It wasn't strange that, at ten years old, we still shared a room: we shared everything. Even more so, now we were poor.

'Come on, sis, I've got something to show you.'

Paul stood on his bed, his blue nylon Aertex underpants pulled tightly round his willy. Tiny bobbles of flesh came through the holes. I ran my fingers across them. Paul took a flying leap across the room, slamming me on the bed. He rammed his foot between my legs and pushed against my minge. 'Submit, submit.'

'Okay, okay. I do,' I said. 'Please, Paulas. You're hurting me.'

They were squatters and we were squatters – we had that much in common.

I watched them as they climbed up on the kitchen roof and through the window. There were three of them: one fair and two dark. The hotel had been empty for years; at the front it was covered with plywood boards, but at the back there were a hundred different windows. And I would watch the windows: it became my obsession. Every glimpse I had of the three men became a secret triumph. I felt they knew I was watching.

I got up early, crept down the stairs and out of the back door. It was daylight and the sun had begun to shine. I was going to see the squatters. They had seen me, I had seen them: they knew I'd been watching. My imagination was filled with them: one fair, two dark. I went through the hole in the wall, and stood beneath their room. The two dark ones – both with long hair, one with a beard – climbed out of the window and stood on the flat roof. 'Hiya,' they said, and smiled. 'You're our watcher.'

I stood there in my pink-and-white-striped nightie, not knowing what to say.

'Does your mum know you're here?'

'No, no one does,' I said. 'You're my secret.'

They reached down and, by my wrists, pulled me up on to the roof. I followed them through the window. The room was square; three lots of sleeping stuff lay on the floor as well as a washing-line, some pots and pans, and a small gas burner. The door to the room was barricaded from the inside.

'What's your name?' The one with the beard asked.

'Tracey. I'm Tracey.'

Smiling, he said, 'Well, pleased to meet you, Tracey. I'm Albert. This here is Bert, and this is Andy.'

They were from a place called Manchester. They had come to Margate for the summer to find work. I liked the way they spoke. It was different. They were different. I stood in my pink-and-white-striped nightie, knowing there might be some danger, but also knowing not to be afraid. They were my secret, almost as though I had invented them: they were the dream of an eleven-year-old girl, my three wise men. And Albert, he looked like Jesus with his long dark hair, full moustache and beard.

Each morning before school, I would creep out of bed, down the stairs, out across the yard, through the hole in the wall and climb on to the roof, sometimes taking them slices of bread, teabags, biscuits – anything I could get from the kitchen without it being noticed. We would play the little radio and, some-times, dance: me, a little girl in my pink-and-white-striped nightie, dancing around a radio with the three wise kings.

They showed me card tricks, and I'd snuggle up in their sleeping stuff while they told me about places I'd never heard of and their lives on the road, the four of us bound in this early-morning secret ritual. Sometimes, when Albert lifted me on to the roof – his arms round my ribs – I would look into his eyes. They were soft and brown with long lashes, gentle like a puppy: like he could never hurt me. I was in love.

School had finished. It was the summer holidays. Mum worked as a chambermaid and would be gone by six thirty each morning.

'You see this coin?' said Albert. 'You can have it if you can roll it all the way down your face, like this.' He held the coin in his hand and, as I watched, he rolled it from the top of his fore-head, down the centre of his nose, across his lips, over his beard and down his neck. I liked it: the silver rolling across his skin.

He passed the coin to Bert and Andy and they did the same. The four of us, cross-legged on the floor, taking part in an ancient ceremony.

'Close your eyes,' said Albert. 'And keep them closed.'

He passed the coin into the palm of my hand and, slowly, I rolled it down the centre of my face.

I opened my eyes, they were laughing and giggling. A big smile spread across my face.

'Christ,' said Albert.

A noise from hell: a pickaxe swung its way through the

door – *smash* – sending bits of wood flying through the air. I was screaming. It seemed as though footsteps and shouts – hundreds of them – were coming from everywhere.

Albert swept me up in his arms, pushed me through the window and, holding my wrist, dropped me from the roof, shouting, '*Run – run – run.*'

I stumbled across the yard, through the hole in the wall and into the arms of a policeman. I wriggled and tried to slip through his hands. My nightie was torn and blood was running down my shins.

I kept my mouth closed and would not tell the police anything. They kept going on and on, but I didn't even listen to them. Then, as Albert, Bert and Andy were taken away in cuffs, I began to cry.

But all the police wanted to know was: how did I get the line?

In a smuttering of tears, I said, 'What line?'

They passed me a mirror and there, from the top of my brow to the bottom of my chin, was a perfect silver line.

And now Paul and I were in the bathroom.

'Look, Tray, I can make it grow.'

He ran his hand up and down his willy. It was getting bigger and bigger. And then – wow – a white spray flew out of the end, splattering across the back of the toilet seat. As he smiled, I stood on the bath, my feet either side of the tub. I picked up the long-handled bath brush and said, 'Well, watch this.'

But, one day, I told Paul I didn't want to do it any more because God would get us.

Paul said, okay, he didn't want to be got by God, because He didn't love us anyway.

Mum was out collecting lead. Since we had squatted the staff cottage, it was easy for her to get into the back of the hotel as it was only boarded up from the front. She didn't believe it was stealing; she felt it was rightfully hers. Me and Paul always got excited by her expeditions: our mum, leaving the house with a hacksaw and shopping-bag. A giant bird gathering food for her chicks. Mum loved us: she would do anything for us.

Strange to think we had been an accident . . .

When my mum was pregnant with me and Paul, people used to spit at her in the street and call her a nigger-lover. Friends tried to persuade her to have an abortion because she wasn't married to our father. Even worse, there might be a throw-back: we might come out black.

When Paul and I first went to school, the other children said our daddy was a wog. We went home and – 'Mummy,' we asked, 'what's a wog?'

She said that if anyone called our father a wog, we should say, 'Yes, a Western Oriental Gentleman.'

Daddy told me that his great-great-grandfather was a slave in the Ottoman empire. A warrior from the Sudan with skin as black as the night. He wore a red fez, rode a great horse and carried a sword by his side.

I no longer have the skin, ride the horse or wear the fez.

But it's good to know that the blood still flows and I still carry the sword by my side.

There were people in our lives who were always coming and going. But Chris seemed to be a permanent fixture.

Something that has always disgusted me . . .

Lying across his lap, I could feel his hard, erect penis pressed into the small of my back and he was rubbing his hands across my chest. My tiny little chest, my bony little ribs. I was only ten.

As I got older, I would watch him from the corner of my eye. His hand down his trousers, always fiddling with himself, always looking at me. Then I would wake in the middle of the night and hear him having sex with Mum. And I'd wake Paul up and say, 'Listen, listen, Paul.'

Paul would say, 'Don't worry, sis. Sis, don't worry.'

It all hurt so much. A stranger coming and going.

The world had become a sad and ugly place.

One day, a kind of warm summer day, my mum was running down the road screaming, 'My baby, my baby, what's wrong with my baby?'

I hung across her arms, my stomach about to explode. I felt my eyes rolling round and my head was gone. I was wearing my pink-and-white-striped nightie, and I remember the yellow of my brother's Chopper bike as he rode down the hill. He was calling, 'Don't worry, sis. Sis, don't worry. I'll get him for you, I'll get him.'

In the hospital, I had to shit into a toilet, and when I went to flush it, I found it didn't have a chain. The toilet had a hole in the bottom where they collected my shit and put it into a little tub. The policewoman was talking to me but I kept kind of sleeping. My auntie was there and she was saying, 'Have you been naughty, mucking around, playing strange games?'

I didn't know what strange games were. To me, it was all part of living. A strange living. I had never known the truth so I had never cared for the truth, rationality or reason. I lived in a world of dreams, good and bad.

I can see myself at nine or ten, walking in the same place again and again. The cliff above me was hundreds of feet high; the air was neither hot nor cold. All I remember is the colour of the sky, that strange blue only seen when day meets night. Twilight time, walking alone for miles and miles. The sea had disappeared: it had been taken away. The land stretched out for ever. Fish lay on the rocks – rocks covered with seaweed and green moss. Everything was still and quiet apart from the white line of the horizon, which began to grow as it drew closer and closer. And with it, a roar; a sound so intense that it killed all other sounds. As it came nearer and nearer, the sky became two different blues, divided by this line. A wave, a wave to end all waves, hundreds of feet high. As it bore down on me, I knew there was no salvation: no ladder or stairway, no wings. I turned towards the cliff, my hands upon my ears, pressing harder and harder. I said, 'Dear God, send it away.' But it didn't go away: the noise was now a thunder.

As though time had slowed down, I turned towards the wave. My eyes had never been so open: I had never seen so much. I would become part of it. As the power of the sea smashed against the weight of the land, my world became black. The wave had gone.

I was left wet and dripping, cold and alone. But excited. I defied the gods.

Now my body stank, every orifice oozing slime, every pore open and closing, every part of me bleeding.

I'm GOING TO GET YOU

YOU CUNT YOU

FUCKING BASTARD.

And when I do — The whole world will Know

That you destroyed Part OF my childhood,

TRACEY Emin.

I stopped eating and took to my bed. I don't know how long this lasted but in my mind it was an eternity. I lived on a diet of orange squash and digestive biscuits. I became thin, pale, short-sighted. My teeth rotted.

My mum brought a new piece of furniture into the house. It was a solid oak cabinet with a platform on top. Hard to describe, but I can see it clearly: Victorian with ball legs and curly carved arms. It was human-size.

One day, my mum came home and found me screaming as I pulled it across the room, 'Get it out of here. Help me get it out.'

I kept seeing a coffin, lying on top of the cabinet with its lid open.

'Get it out of here. Please, help me. Get it out.'

The next day my mum had it removed.

She worked night and day – God, did she save – so that we could go on the school trip. It was 3 January 1974. We were being taken to Austria to ski in the Tyrol. Five of us girls slept in a dorm-style room. On the first night, I had a chill in my stomach. I went to bed: soon, the bed was saturated. I lay there in the damp coldness of my own piss.

In the morning I said I didn't feel too well – too afraid to leave my bed, afraid of my secret. As the last girl left the room, I began to tear the white cotton yellow-stained sheet into thin strips and stuff them into my bag.

For the next nine days, I smuggled a little of the sheet

out of my room and up into the mountains. As the others ski'd and played, I disappeared to bury my secret in the white snow.

Mum was at the Gay Nights, a nightclub in Ramsgate where she worked. Sometimes she'd take Paul and me, and while she waited on the tables, we would curl up on the red-velvet sofas, drifting off to sleep to the sound of Isaac Hayes in the background. And at two or three in the morning, when the last customer had gone, we'd both be carried into the taxi for the journey home.

On other nights, she would leave us at home, alone.

I sat up in bed, the night's silence burning my mind, the covers pulled up close around my face, lying in my own piss, too scared to breathe, my eyes darting around the semi-darkness.

Paul lay asleep in his bed on the other side of the room.

'Psst, psst, Paul. Listen, Paul, wake up. There's someone downstairs.'

The house was creaking, creaking like it was alive. As though it was breathing. Everything chilled; the air became ice.

'Paul, Paul. Wake up.'

I could hear footsteps coming up the stairs towards the kitchen. *Smash* – a glass. A cup. The bang of a chair.

I couldn't move. I lay there motionless. The footsteps, the creaking of the floorboards becoming louder.

There was no door to our bedroom. All that separated me from the footsteps was a golden curtain . . . and it moved.

The darkness became more dark, more dense. I felt the press of a hundred million atoms as it swept over me like a black sea.

The window! I could get out of the window. With frenzied little hands, I forced it open. And as Mum's taxi pulled up outside, I was there, screaming hysterically, 'Save me! Help me, Mummy! Mummy, please!'

All the lights were turned on. The house was searched. I told them it had come from the basement but, of course, they couldn't find anything.

We don't look for death: it finds us.

And then it was okay. I shared a room with my mum and I felt safe. The warm smell of her, her perfume, her makeup, her clothes. Mum was now working at the Roxburgh, a hotel round the corner, as a chambermaid, and on Saturdays I would help her, cleaning out the rooms and carrying the laundry baskets.

I had started eating and stopped wetting the bed. It seemed like we were happy, that all the evil had gone. Although, apart from Maria, I didn't really have any friends. And I was still very thin and yellow-looking, an ugly little thing. I needed glasses and my teeth were really fucked. The boys used to say they had seen more fat on a chip. I had no tits, no hips, and I only ate digestive biscuits.

Paul had gone to Mark Golding's house and I was alone, friendless on another hot summer day.

Mum made me some sandwiches, cheese and tomato, and I put them in my bag along with my towel and my bikini.

Off I went to the beach. It was the height of the summer season and Margate was packed. The Golden Mile was speckled with a thousand million people. I made my way across the sand to the sundeck where I found a little space on the wooden planks and unpacked my bag. My bikini top was gone. My black, wet-look fringy bikini top: not there! And I had walked miles – I could have lost it anywhere.

I sat down in the heat. There was nothing for it: I would have to swim without my top. Putting two fingers across my nipples, I made my way to the water's edge.

Ooh, it was cold. The little waves lapped against my feet. It felt nice. And as I rolled around, I thought, I love the sea.

Some other kids were playing close by. They had a giant rubber ring. I watched longingly as they all jumped and splashed and laughed. And then, to my amazement, they beckoned me over. Me, I thought. They're calling me!

I splashed my way over to them in excitement. And as I hoisted myself out of the water and up on to the rubber ring, one of them said, 'See? I told you she was a boy.'

'Are you a boy or a girl?' one of the other kids said.

'A girl,' I said. 'I'm a girl.'

There were about six of them. They pushed me through the centre of the ring and bundled on top of me. Below the water, I could hear them chanting, *Boy, boy, boy, boy.*

Later, I sat on the sundeck with my towel wrapped round me, like a little nun, only my face poking out.

The clock tower struck five. People began to leave the beach in droves. It was time for the evening meal for those staying in hotels, train time for the day-trippers.

I opened my sandwiches. They were sweaty and the toma-toes had made the bread go soggy. I thought, Wish my Mum was at home. And I began to cry.

In tears, I pulled myself along the now empty beach, my feet dragging through the sand. A voice said, 'What's wrong, little girl?'

It came from a big, brown hairy man. I started to blubber even more, telling him my whole story. He made me laugh and smile. He told me I was beautiful. He gently covered the whole of my body with tiny golden grains of sand. And in the water, he ran his hands all over me. He said I was like a tiny mermaid and, for me, he was like a giant bear. And I pulled at his willy until a giant spray of white covered my limbs.

I wasn't yet twelve, but I knew it could feel lovely to be a girl.

A young girl sits in bed, crocheting by a small light, furi-ously, one stitch after another. She looks at the clock: five minutes to one.

She jumps out of bed, puts on her slippers and her coat over her nightdress. Quietly, she goes down to the kitchen window. There, in the darkness and the rain, the light of a torch shines. It moves three times.

She lets herself out of the back door. Ryan is there, waiting. Without a sound they make their way down to the bottom of the garden to the shed.

She is twelve, Ryan is eighteen. He's been homeless for three or four months; his father's an alcoholic and has always beaten him. They curl up in the shed and look at the stars through the skylight. He kisses her forehead; she strokes the back of his neck. She is tiny compared to him, yet she's protecting him.

In the morning, the first light of day, he is lying on top of her, kissing her passionately. She is saying that she will always love him for his kindness and begs him to make love to her. But he won't: he says he's a virgin and that she's too young. But he wants something to remember her by for ever.

He kneels, half naked, and hands her a bottle of Indian ink and a razor blade. She starts to carve her initials into the back of his calf.

They're both laughing, oblivious of being watched. When she has finished – blood and ink flowing down his leg, black smears under her nails – she kisses the back of his neck, and says, 'I've got to go now.'

I had friends now, and every Saturday night, the girls would stay, four of us in my single bed: two tops, two tails. Cindy and Lisa at one end, me and Lindsay at the other.

Lisa wasn't a virgin any more: she and Keith had done it lots of times. She showed us her love bites – they went from her knees to the top of her thighs and from her stomach to her neck, a trail of purple and blue puffy bruises with faint yellow rings. Cindy said she liked to have her tits rubbed, I said I didn't like to be touched at all, and Lindsay said she liked to put red lipstick on her nipples and play with her love button. Lindsay and Cindy swore allegiance to remain virgins until the day they married. I swore to be a virgin until the day I died.

We were only thirteen but it was hot and exciting.

I lost one of my front teeth in the cloakroom. I was eating a sweet and my tooth just crumbled into dust. The dentist put a cap on it but it never stayed, even though I used to glue it in with Poly-grip. In the end, I just walked around with a gap, a hand over my mouth.

I didn't blame Paul for head-butting me and smashing my other front tooth: I never smiled that much anyway. It was just before Christmas. The dentist, Mr Goldberg, decided to give me a denture: *false teeth*. And two days before Christmas I smiled for the first time in months. Mum bought me some new clothes – a petrol blue mac and a pair of gold star earrings. It was the best Christmas I'd ever had. And on New Year's Eve I went to Top Spot, the Sunday night disco for over-sixteens. Everyone from Margate was going. I danced to 'The Hustle', 'Young Hearts Run Free' and Queen. When I smiled, people said my teeth looked good.

At eleven fifteen, I decided to go home, spend New Year's Eve with my mum and Paul. I left Top Spot and walked along the sea-front. All the lights were on and the world felt like magic. Margate looked like Las Vegas.

Steve Worrell called after me, 'Tracey, where are you going?'

He walked along with me. We passed the clock tower and turned left into the high street. He slipped his arm round my shoulders and said, 'How about a New Year kiss?'

We got to the corner of Burton's shoe shop and started

snogging. He put his hand down my top, at the same time pushing me against the wall. He pulled my skirt up. I began to worry. Everyone knew he had broken in girls before and I didn't want it to happen to me. I said, 'No. Get off, please.'

He pulled me down the alley and pushed me to the ground. As I lay on my back worrying about my new blue coat, he pushed his fingers up between my legs – and rammed himself into me.

I was crying. His lips were pressed against mine but I was motionless, like a small corpse. He grunted and I knew it was over. He got up, I just lay there on the ground, my tights round my ankles. The clock was striking twelve.

As he walked away, he turned and said, 'I've always wanted to do it to you. I like your mouth.'

When I got in, my mum said, 'Tracey, what's wrong with you?'

I showed her my coat, the dirt and the stains, and told her, 'I'm not a virgin any more.'

She didn't call the police or make any fuss. She just washed my coat and everything carried on as normal, as though nothing had happened. But for me, my childhood was over, I had become conscious of my physicality, aware of my presence and open to the ugly truths of the world. At the age of thirteen, I realised that there was a danger in innocence and beauty, and I could not live with both.

Postscript

I was seven years old.

'Mummy,' I said. 'One of the girls in my class, it's her

birthday and this evening she's having a party. Can I go?'

I put on my favourite party dress. Mum carefully wrapped some cheap Turkish jewellery in a piece of tissue paper for my gift. And up the road I went. Outside school, five or six girls stood around. The birthday girl arrived with her dad in the car, and as everybody went to get in, the girl said, 'You can't come.'

Her father followed her, saying sternly, 'I'm afraid you're not invited. You don't have an invitation.'

I waited outside school for as long as I could. Then I hid the jewellery, I went home. Mum asked, 'Did you enjoy the party?'

I said, 'Yes, it was lovely.'

That night, I lay in bed and cried. I cried myself to sleep. And in the morning, I asked, 'Mummy, what's an invitation?'

Dear Uncle Colin

When you left the house that winter morning and you said to Mum, 'When I die, I want them to play "Lay Lady Lay" by Bob Dylan at my funeral', did you know you were never coming back?

And now, dear Uncle Colin, what's left of you? These two photographs: the one of you looking like Peter Sellers with your first car, and the other taken twenty years later, looking out to sea.

You were always my favourite uncle. You wrote love poetry and did the Tarot cards. And when Mum was pregnant with me and Paul and decided to have an abortion, you waited outside the clinic, hoping she would change her mind.

The little seagull you and Mum found while walking along the beach barefoot – you both agreed it was lucky.

The silver puzzle box you kept on the dashboard of your car and that you used to play with all the time.

And a packet of Benson and Hedges, slightly crushed. I guess they were the last thing you ever held.

When they told me you were dead, I wasn't surprised. I went upstairs quietly and ran a bath. I didn't cry. The story of how you died filled me with horror. But I still didn't cry – because deep in my soul I know the soul can endure.

Where Do I Go Now?

It's a strange thing when you come from a place – or, rather, when you have somehow created the place that you came from. The Margate of my mind has the most beautiful sunsets that stretch across the entire horizon. Sharp white cliffs divide a charcoal blue sea from the hard reality of the land.

Margate – the nub of the Isle of Thanet, thrusting like a bent forefinger from the crazed knuckle of England. A Hades Paradise, famed for times long gone. Planet Thanet, also known as the Last Resort. Frankie Howerd, Danny La Rue, Norman Wisdom . . . they all played here. One of my teenage claims to fame is that I danced on stage with the one and only Mr Chuck Berry at the Margate Winter Gardens. The

Winter Gardens: it sounds like the name of a romantic Victorian graveyard.

Margate's never been easy, always hard. 'If you want a dirty weekend, go to Margate,' I always say. You can be as dirty as you like. Van Gogh and Turner, Ronnie Biggs and the Krays all went there. Romans, Vikings, Hell's Angels, teds, mods, rockers and punks, they all fought there.

In 1977, when the punks came to town, me and my friend Maria were working in the Garden Café, Dreamland. Dreamland – a wild Victorian fun-fair where the Catch-a-duck and Shoot-a-coconut mixed with the sounds of the Wurlitzer and Eddie Cochran. Elvis had just died, but we were rock-and-roll Buddy Hollys, with shades of David Bowie, in our hand-made drainpipe jeans, dyed red hair and Azootec T-shirts. Thirteen years old, without a care in the world. It was the year of the Queen's Silver Jubilee and our job was to clean the food off the Garden Café's three hundred tables. People came in and ate their food, then we cleared away the scraps of eggs, beans, chips, sausage and mash. A bilge of greasy hell scraped by bare hands into a giant industrial canteen trolley.

Why they called it the Garden Café I will never know, but opposite was the Bali-hi, a strange Hawaiian drinking bar left over from the 1950s; a ghostly haunt of long gone GIs. Elvis lookalikes came to sing their last songs, families sat in tears now that the King was dead.

One day, a man wearing bondage trousers and a butcher's apron covered with blood stood in front of my boss and, pointing at me, said, 'She's coming with us.'

I spent the next three hours being called Baby Punk as they took me on the roller-coaster, the dodgems and the scenic railway. I was cradled in the arms of a giant punk family, who acted as though they were wild baby-sitters. I was dropped off promptly at six o'clock at the Garden Café with the words, 'And she'll get paid for it.' And I did: the boss paid me a full day's wages.

It was *Kidnap on the Isle of Thanet*, except that I wasn't a kid. I was thirteen: I had been raped, I had lost my front teeth and I had suffered disillusionment with life. But I knew there was something better: there was an outside – an outside of me. And somewhere that wasn't Margate.

Yet I owe so much to the place I grew up, mainly because it is so beautiful. And what is so fantastic and beautiful is the sunset, and that is free.

Like a Fucking Dog: When
the Truth is Hard to Bear

I waved goodbye to my mum at the school gates: it wasn't her fault that I smoked. As I walked back round to the girls' cloakrooms, Angelica Smart came scuttering up beside me. Angelica Smart, what a name. She was far from angelic: she was fat and sweaty, a bit greasy on the centre parting. And almost friendless. Most of the other kids felt sorry for her because her mum had died.

'Tracey, was that your mum I saw you with? What happened about the smoking?'

'Nothing,' I said. 'My mum knows I smoke. She gives me the odd fag here and there.'

'Wow,' said Angelica. 'I always thought you'd have a cool mum. But I didn't think she'd be old.'

Suddenly the whole world stood still. The clouds froze, the blossom stopped swaying and I screwed up my face. 'At least I've got a fucking mum.'

Before Angelica could reply, I pushed her down the bank, with one almighty shove. She rolled like a lump of dough and smashed into the cherry tree.

As I said, Angelica didn't have too many friends. But she did have her cousin Suzy Smart. Me and Maria came out of class to find a huge crowd had gathered on the field by the old flint huts. Angelica was there, waiting, with Suzy by her side. Suzy Smart wasn't big, but she was butch. Butch like a boy: a hard boy, with muscles and a thick jaw. When we all got tits, her voice broke.

There was no way I was going to get out of this. They weren't letting me pass.

'What's up, Suze?' I said. 'Your willy not grown yet?'

Everybody laughed.

'Shagged any girls lately? Or are you too busy playing football with the boys?'

Her fist came flying into my face. It felt like a fucking hammer.

I wobbled a little and turned my head. I said, 'Oh, yeah, lesbo. Let's see you do that again.'

And she did – *crack*.

Everyone was shouting, *Fight – fight – fight!*

Coolly I took off my blazer, removed my front false teeth and passed them to Maria, who stood at my side.

Before she had time to hit me again, I grabbed Suzy: one hand holding her hair, the other tight on her collar. And as the bright spring light shone down, I summoned all the gods and smashed her face into the flint wall. Again and again and again. Blood squirted everywhere. The shouts of '*Fight*', had stopped. Other girls were trying to pull me off, but they couldn't. I was like a wild, senseless animal, and Suzy Smart had become nothing.

Finally, she fell to the floor: a sobbing blubbery mess. Yellow lumps the size of eggs began to appear on her head.

Walking away, I pulled my socks back up and tucked my shirt back in.

Then, turning, I shouted, 'That will teach you. No one – absolutely no one – calls my mum old.'

Falling Asleep With My Eyes Open

That high-pitched tone. I'm half sweating, half shivering, curled up tight into a ball and clinging to the radiator. I'm angry with myself. I push the alarm-clock button with my finger and the tone stops. The room bleeds into darkness.

I go to the bathroom, brush my teeth and slosh some water over my swollen face. My clothes feel stuck to me. I smell of decay, the acrid smell of a lonely person, a person with no respect or regard for themselves.

I get into my very large bed, with its puffy duvet and four soft pillows. My head sinks into them. It's five a.m. and I wonder why I didn't do this six hours ago. What is it that stops me going to bed? Ever since I can remember, as I was lifted and carried to my bed, I have fallen asleep with my eyes open.

He is standing next to the bed, bare feet, red boxer shorts, cheeky-looking. He beckons me to follow him into the hall, gesturing with his hand as he half smiles. There is a blackness to his eyes, not like his real eyes. But I want him, I want to go with him. I pull back the covers. In my nakedness, I follow him out of the room but the hallway has gone and, instead, we are standing on a sea wall, the shape of a dam. We look out to sea. It's beautiful. I can smell the Mediterranean.

'Christ.'

I cry out as he plunges a knife into my stomach, over and over. The sea is begging to disappear. Blood is pumping into my hands, hot and sticky.

My eyes open. I am holding my stomach, gripping myself and breathing madly. My whole body heaves uncontrollably. I turn on the light, jump out of bed and run into the hall. He's gone. The fucking bastard: tricked by my own loneliness, and it fucking knew.

Sometimes I don't fall for it. I wise up to it, even in my sleep, though it comes in many guises. When I was young it would come as pure energy, a dark mask that would float above me. But now it's clever: it comes as Mark Pearson.

I was thirteen, he was fourteen. We'd been round Dreamland together. He'd followed me into the Sphinx, the Egyptian house of horror. It was a dark maze of corridors, each one leading to a room that offered a different fear: mirrors, soft floors, mummies that appeared from nowhere, dangly hands that dropped suddenly from the ceiling, and the sound of the wind blowing across the desert. It was so dark, and in the darkness I felt him. He pushed me with the weight of his body against the soft foam walls, our feet began to sink into the sand. We were kissing, kissing passionately, whispering. He was breathing into my ear, breathing into my mouth, giving me his breath and taking mine. He held my neck, he ran his hands all over my body, hardly touching me. He told me I was beautiful. He told me he was going to join the French Foreign Legion.

He told me, 'One day, I'll say "I love you" in French.'

We lay in his mum and dad's bed on a hot August Saturday afternoon. He was holding me wrapped in his arms, kissing me. It felt so safe. I would believe every word he said.

Have you ever longed for someone so much, so deeply that you thought you would die? That your heart would just stop beating? I am longing now, but for whom I don't know. My whole body craves to be held. I am desperate to love and be loved. I want my mind to float into another's. I want to be set free from despair by the love I feel for another. I want to be physically part of someone. I want to be joined. I want to be open and free to explore every part of them, as though I were exploring myself.

I want to go to sleep and wake with my skin taut. I want to feel cum on my face. I want to laugh with my eyes open.

I want to sleep with my eyes closed.

When I was 14 - 15
There was nothing to my life
        but dancing and sex
I'd go to night clubs and dance
Then I'd meet someone and have sex
        It was Fine and easy
            nothing to do
BUT Think with my body
        like a bird
    I Thought I was Free

                        Tracey Emin

Nayland Rock

A girl dances provocatively; she's no more than thirteen or fourteen. It's Margate, 1977. She's dancing to 'Cocaine in my Brain'.

Freddy, a black–Chinese guy, the town's number-one drugs-dealer, watches her. He is Margate's cool guy: she's had a crush on him for weeks. She knows he's watching her.

Freddy grabs her by the wrist – out of the disco and along the sea-front – referring to her as a *bitch*.

He takes her to the Nayland Rock Hotel. They check into a room; he jacks up with more speed.

He tries to fuck her. He's pathetic. His cock is soft and small.

The girl thinks, Is this all there is to Freddy?

He passes out on the bed, half naked. The girl looks at the clock: it's three a.m. There's a phone by the bed so she calls her mum and says, 'I'm safe, I'm on my way home.'

On her way out, she goes through Freddy's pockets, takes sixteen pounds, a gold lighter and twenty Benson and Hedges. Closing the door, she thinks, That will teach him to be shit in bed.

Hades

A young girl is dancing at a provincial disco – to 'Wishing On A Star' – dancing in a very provocative way. It's hard to say how old she is, sixteen or seventeen at the very most, but in a certain light she might almost seem nineteen or twenty.

A good-looking guy in his mid-twenties is watching her. As a group of women begin line-dancing, he asks the girl if she wants a drink. They go to the bar; she sips her Pernod and blackcurrant. He can't take his eyes off her breasts.

Suddenly a fight breaks out: chairs, glasses, bottles fly. The lights go on and the police storm the place.

The guy grabs the girl's hand and takes her out of the club

through the back exit. She wraps her arms round herself, and says, 'It's cold.' She is wearing a glittery boob-tube, tight black velvet trousers and silver mules. He offers her his jacket.

'No,' she says, then: 'Where to now?'

They are walking towards a car park. He points to a red Ford van. His name is Pete Smiles and he is twenty-three. He's engaged, but he is fascinated by the girl. He asks her how old she is? *Sixteen? Seventeen?*

'Fourteen,' she replies.

He says he knows it's wrong. The van has a mattress in the back and, without saying very much more, he pushes her in and fucks her furiously.

Afterwards, they drive to a fish-and-chip shop. He buys her a bag of chips, then drives her to the end of her street. She gets out of the van, with the chips in her hand.

And as he drives off, she puts it down as possibly the best sex she's ever had.

Why I Never Became A Dancer

I never liked school
I was always late anyway.
In fact, I hated it
so I left at thirteen.

I'd hang around cafés drinking coffee,
exploring Margate's Golden Mile:
The clock tower,
the cafés and bars,
Polises,
The Bali-hi.
Lunchtime disco.

Drinking cider,
lying out on the beach.

The summers were amazing,
nothing to do but dream.
It was ideal.
And there was sex,
it was something you could just do
and it was free.

Sex was something simple.
You'd go to a pub, walk home,
have fish and chips, then sex
on the beach,
down alleys,
greens,
parks.
Even hotels.

It didn't matter that I was young
thirteen, fourteen.
It didn't matter that they were men of
nineteen, twenty, twenty-five, twenty-six.
It never crossed my mind to ask them
what the attraction was.
I knew
sex was what it was.

And it could be good,

really something.
I remember the first time someone
asked me to grab their balls,
I remember the power it gave me

But it wasn't always like that.
Sometimes they'd just cum
and leave me there – where I was,
half naked.

But there were no morals, rules
or judgements.
I did just what I wanted to do.

By the time I was fifteen, I'd had them all,
and for me Margate was too small,
and I knew the difference between
good and bad.
The reason why these men wanted to fuck me –
a fourteen-year-old girl –
was because they weren't men.
They were pathetic.
Sex for me had been an adventure
a learning, an innocence.
A wild escape from
all the shit that surrounded me.

I stopped shagging
but I was still flesh

and I still thought with my body.

But now it was different –
it was me and dancing.

That's where I got my real kick,
out on the dance-floor.
It felt like I could defy gravity.
As though my soul were
truly free.

Then the big one came:
the local finals.
If I won I'd be up there,
London, the Empire, Leicester Square
dancing for TV and big prizes.
The British Disco Dance Championship, 1978.

And as I started to dance,
people started to clap.
I was going to win
and then I was out of here.
Nothing could stop me.
And then they started:
'*SLAG, SLAG, SLAG.*'
A gang of blokes, most of whom I'd had sex with
at some time or other
started to chant.
The chant became louder –

'*SLAG, SLAG, SLAG*' –
until in the end I couldn't hear
the music any more
or the people clapping.
My head was spinning
and I was crying.
I'd lost it.
I ran off the dance-floor,
out of the club,
down the steps to the sea.

And I thought, I'm leaving this place,
I'm out of here.
I'm better than all of them.
I'm free.
So I left Margate
I left all those boys
Wayne –
Freddy –
Tony –
Doug –
Richard –

This one's for you.

Art and Life a Very Thin Line
Like the Curve of a Heart

I was back in Margate. I looked across the harbour wall and, for a moment, I saw us all as kids: me, Paul, the Pettman brothers, Maria, Janette, Nikki and Joe. The Beach Boys booming in our minds, the hot summer sun, the tide up high. Jumping off the harbour wall, defying the waves and our fear of being dragged out to sea. Christ, life had been good. Now I was seventeen. I wondered what had happened to that wild ambition. I'd lived in London for two years: how come I was back?

The eighties started for me in a DHSS bed-and-breakfast, fourteen pounds a week, eating Pot Noodle and Kentucky

Fried Chicken. I had left school early – well, as early as I could – at fifteen, although Paul and I had stopped going at thirteen, for entirely different reasons. Paul had lost the palm of his left hand in an accident at the local bowling alley, while I had discovered men, sex and nightclubs. At fifteen I went back to school and sat a few CSEs, one in drama. Surprisingly I did quite well: I won an award. Then I went straight to London.

I left with twenty pounds, a holdall with some clothes and two David Bowie LPs. I stayed all over the place – floors, squats, cupboards – met all kinds of people and had all kinds of jobs, mainly retail, clothes and shoes. I stuck it as long as I could.

Then one day I felt tired, lonely, cold, and wanted to feel safe. I just wanted to go home, to my mum. So I went back to Margate: back to where the sun shone.

But it was winter: the sun wasn't shining. My mum had sold the house, or it was taken away. She was now living in Barnet, and all our things were in storage. So I ended up in a DHSS bed-and-breakfast, down Athelston Road. I never once had a bath there. I used to boil a kettle and stand in a bowl. I had an ancient two-bar electric fire. It was horrible: I could never call that home. KFC – the Kentucky Fried Chicken shop – that was home for a long time.

I had to get out, which meant I had to get a job: any job. I walked down the high street and there it was in big, gaping letters – *Shop Assistant Wanted*. I went in.

A creepy-looking man behind the counter asked if he could help.

I said, 'I need a job.'

Staring at my tits, he asked how old I was.

'Seventeen,' I told him.

'Do you know much about this kind of stuff?'

'No. But I'm sure I could pick it up.' I looked about me: dildos, vibrators, girlie mags, finger bobs, sexy underwear – red and black nylon, bits of frilly lace.

'One pound an hour,' he said. 'And you start now.'

I asked if he paid cash in hand, and that was it. I had myself a job.

I had just started reading – books, that is – so most of the day I would sit behind the counter reading, about Hollywood, mainly: David Niven, Marilyn Monroe, Frank Sinatra, Greta Garbo, Cecil B. de Mille. Occasionally I would serve someone. Sometimes I would rearrange displays. At lunch, I would buy a double vanilla cone from Mario's and eat it sitting on the harbour wall. I'd watch the birds, so graceful, so beautiful, their wings spread out against the blue.

I walked back in to work.

'Ah, you're back, Tracey. This is a friend of mine. He's a photographer. An artist. An artistic photographer. He's also a very talented hypnotist.'

The photographer smiled at me. His front teeth were missing and his tongue slipped through the gap.

'He'd like to take some photos of you.'

'Why?'

'He'll pay you.'

'How much?' I asked.

'Six pounds.'

The photographer smiled again. I was handed a fistful of underwear and told to go upstairs.

There was a striped mattress on the floor and a sheet had been hung across the window. I took off my clothes and put on the first things that came to hand: a black tasselly bra and a red nylon heart-shaped G-string. I could hear them coming upstairs.

'Stand in the corner, love. Put your hands above your head. Chest out.'

'Isn't she lovely? Look at those brown curves. She's Turkish, and you know what they say: full of eastern promise.'

'Tracey, love, relax. Take your bra off. That's right, love. Don't be shy.'

I posed a few more times and the photographer took a few more shots. Then, slowly, he walked towards me and lowered his hand towards the red heart shape.

'What are you doing?' I snapped, putting my hand across my fanny.

'Relax, love. Relax. There was just something hanging down. I was only going to tuck it in. I'm an artist, remember.'

'Yeah,' I said. 'And so am I. And if you don't mind, I can tuck it in myself, thanks.'

At the end of the day, there was forty-eight quid in the till. I wanted to take it, but didn't. Instead, I told the boss, 'I'm quitting. You can find someone else to work in your sleazy shit-hole. And another thing – if that film of me isn't destroyed, I'll make sure I destroy you.'

That evening back in my DHSS bed-and-breakfast, I wrote a letter:

Dear Margate Police Station

I am an artist. When the weather is good, I often go out sketching. Over the last few weeks I have noticed a number of young women going into the sex shop. I do not know what goes on, but I am suspicious enough to know that it should be investigated.

Yours sincerely

ANONYMOUS

A year or so later, my mum returned to Margate. We got a flat together above the Kentucky Fried Chicken shop and I managed to get a place at college. One night there was a knock on the door: it was the police and they wanted to talk to me. It was confidential, they said. They were from the Vice Squad. They'd been tipped off about the sex shop and when they'd raided the place, they'd found my name and previous address.

They showed me hundreds of contact sheets of girls – young girls, some I knew from school. At least six or seven were in explicit poses, some having sex. The police said they wanted to nail the bastard and needed to know if there were any photos of me.

I told them my story. The police asked why I'd done it. 'For six quid, of course. Why else?' I said.

The officer put his hand on my shoulder and said, 'You seem like quite an intelligent girl to me. If I was you, I'd go down to this shop, when it's dark one night, and throw a brick through the window.'

I closed the door on them.

My mum asked who it was. I said, 'Oh, nothing. Just the police.'

Two weeks later, I left Margate for good. Still clutching my heart, safe and intact.

Postscript

If any of you go down to Margate, do me a favour: throw a brick from me.

Someone's Going To Die For This

When I was twenty, I went to Margate by train. I left my flat in Rochester, drunk and crying. All I took with me was a note and half a bottle of whisky. I staggered off the train, knowing not a soul in the world, or where I was, or where I was going.

The sky above was a deep blue. I sat on the harbour wall, staring at the lights, The clock tower struck eleven. The black sea rolled by beneath me. I said, 'Goodbye' and threw myself off the harbour wall, fully clothed, the note in my pocket.

I sank beneath the water and, like a cork, popped back up. The sea became my bed as I floated around for a while, a tiny part of this great world and more alive than ever.

Slowly, I swam to the harbour wall and hoisted myself on to the ladder. I climbed up it. And, in my sodden state, I walked away.

An Ounce of Gold

We both sat there – Victoria station – with cups of tea. She put her hands up to her face, covering her eyes, and said, 'Tray, what are we going to do?'

I emptied out my pockets. I had one pound seventy-five. 'It's all I've got,' I said. 'You have it.' I told her to get some cigarettes.

'But you're in a hurry. You keep it, dear. Get yourself something to eat.'

I looked at her. 'Please, please, don't cry. I'll be all right.'

She held my hand and said, 'If only we could go home.'

But where was home? I'd had no home for months now, and that had been nothing but a small room, with everything

I owned crammed into it. An electric kettle, sachet soups and Pot Noodle.

I squeezed her hand. 'We'll think of something.'

She let go. She raised her hands to her neck, loosened her scarf and carefully removed her gold chain. On it hung a small gold bar, an ounce of gold. She placed it in my hands.

'Sell,' she told me. She was crying.

I ran out of the station with the gold in my palm. I crossed the bus station. On the other side, crammed between the sandwich shops, a pawn-shop sign hung above a doorway. I walked in and handed over the gold.

'Twenty quid is the best I can do,' the man told me.

'Twenty-five,' I said.

He checked and weighed it, then handed over the cash. I ran back to the station. She was still sitting there in a trance. As she looked up, I smiled and handed her the twenty-five pounds. She opened my hand and placed a ten-pound and five-pound note in the palm, saying, 'I love you, dear.'

As she disappeared into the London crowd, I felt alone again. But I understood her: I respected and admired her.

'And,' I shouted above the crowd, 'I love you. I love you Mum. MUM, I LOVE YOU.'

The Greatest Love of My Mum's Life

I came in late. The flat was quiet. I opened my mum's bedroom door. She and Margarete were sound asleep, curled up close together like a little ball.

Sometimes I used to say to my mum, 'Mum, you can tell me. Are you and Margarete lovers? You can tell me. Are you lesbians?' My mum looked at me as if to say, 'Don't be stupid.'

Margarete used to phone my mum every day. Maybe three or four times a day. When she was drunk, she would phone my mum non-stop. They would speak to each other in baby German, calling each other Baby Rabbit and Love.

When I was fourteen, my mum sort of left home to live with Margarete.

Margarete was a psychiatric nurse. She lived in the nurses' wing of Friern Barnet mental hospital. Margarete was Austrian. When she was young, she married a very rich Jew. He was a lot older than her, and when he died he left Margarete everything. Margarete didn't have much to do with her family in Austria. For years, her only real relationship was with my mum.

At first it was okay. In fact, it was fine. Even when Margarete got drunk and started calling my dad a dirty Turk and kind of flipped out of her head and became a blue-eyed Fascist monster, it was still all right.

My mum loved her.

Once when she came to stay, she got drunk and went missing. I had to go and find her. She was in a hotel, drunk out of her mind and crying like a little girl. I carried her home to my mum.

That was okay: I always understood. But in the September of 1992, I was in a bad way. I went home to be with my mum. I'd had an abortion early in the year and I thought I had got over it okay – but I hadn't. You never do. I felt alone; I wanted my mum. I felt dangerous to myself, leaving a trail of destruction and chaos and emotional decay wherever I went.

So I went to my mum's.

Margarete was there. I was behaving like an out-of-control maniac. My mum said to me, 'There, Tracey. Your eyes are flashing.'

I looked at Margarete – I hated her. I hated her. She demanded so much of my mum.

I said to Mum, 'Either I leave or Margarete does.' It turned out that we both stayed, for three days, saying nothing to each other. My mum cried until I went back to London.

She came to the station with me. She told me that Margarete was retiring from work and would move in with her until she found a place of her own. I told my mum, 'As long as Margarete lives with you, I'll never come back to the flat.'

Months went by. I never went to see my mum. Then, just before Christmas, I received a letter from her saying that Margarete wasn't very well. She was in a lot of pain and was having difficulty walking. 'Please, Tray,' she wrote. 'Just try and be nice to Margarete for my sake.'

I felt bad and guilty. I wrote Margarete a letter, explaining how I felt: how I was jealous, and probably always would be of her and mum's relationship. I wrote that it was hard not to be the most important woman in my mum's life. But, I said, Margarete had been a part of my life since I was fourteen and deep down I loved her.

It was just that I was jealous.

Margarete phoned me. She was coming to London. We arranged to meet at Victoria station. We both drank a pint of beer and, over an hour, we talked it all through. Afterwards, I took her to the platform to see her on to the return train. I hugged her. I was so happy. She was lovely, really. She asked if there was anything I wanted or needed.

I laughed and said, 'Just remember me in your will.'

As the train pulled out, she was waving through the window. I can still see her as the train curved around the track and disappeared.

I never saw Margarete again. Six months later she died of bone cancer – she died in my mum's arms. She and mum had been close for sixteen years.

Actually, I did see Margarete one more time – in a dream. It was a funeral, for my mother. It was in an old school hall. Hundreds of people were there, sad and crying. Margarete sat at a table, wearing a sky blue nurse's uniform. She was very thin and her blonde hair was now white. She sat with her back to everybody.

I entered the hall late. Margarete stared up at me, blue eyes like diamonds. I knew she hated me but she said nothing. Her look said it all: she hated me.

I never understood: Margarete made no will. Her body was sent back to Austria and she left my mum nothing.

A few summers ago, I found a photo of me eating a plate of cheese and pickle sandwiches. I remembered that Margarete had taken it. On the back, she had written:

August 1978
To Dear Lovely Tracy
Just how I remember you,
Love Margarete
xx

And I cried and cried and cried and cried and cried. Dear Margarete, forgive me. All my love, Tracey.

For Joseph Samuels

The first time I met Joe Sammy – I remember it clearly – I was twelve, staring out of the youth-club window, miles away, lost in a world of my own. Joe came up behind me and grabbed at my bottom. My first period had started and what Joe grabbed was a handful of sanitary towel. We both stood there motionless.

'Please, Joe, please don't tell anyone,' I said.

He smiled, big long tombstone teeth. 'So what?' he said. 'You're on the rag.'

It's funny, he never did tell anyone. It remained our secret. I always like Joe for that.

*   *   *

Paul stood in front of me, tears running down his face. 'I've got to go to the police, sis. I've got to tell them what I know.'

I hated it when Paul cried. Not because I felt sorry for him, but being twins we always felt each other's pain.

Joe had been missing for two days. No one had seen him. He'd kind of vanished off the face of the earth – a difficult thing to do in Margate, a derelict seaside town where there was nothing to do but blend in with the general decay: bum around, fuck, be fucked, fight and wish your life away.

Paul and Joe had spent the summer lazing around on the green near the clock tower. You could always find them there, drinking cocktails of whisky and cider. Joe in the sta-Prest Ben Sherman, braces and boots, Paul with his bleached-blond Mohican, dog collar and leather gear. Both eighteen, looking good. Always flash with pockets full of money, selling hand-fuls of blues to anyone interested.

The last day Paul and Joe spent together they had got into a few scraps – it was to be expected in Margate. Hordes of day-trippers would roll off the trains looking for adventure. Fighting was part of that.

But this day was different. Paul and Joe had been getting non-stop hassle from a gang of marines – big ugly hard-cases. The day was really heavy.

It was early evening. Paul and Joe sat on the harbour wall. The air was heavy and the greenflies were out. There was going to be a storm.

Paul and Joe popped a few blues and decided to go their separate ways.

Three days later, Joe's body was washed up on Margate

beach: puffy, bloated, unrecognisable. His black skin had turned white. Apparently his fingernails had been smashed and every bone in his hands had been broken.

At the inquest, there was never any real explanation for this. Everybody knew that Joe couldn't swim. It was easy to give a verdict of death by misadventure. Paul always believed the marines had done it.

Paul and I cried together as we imagined Joe's last moments: clinging to the harbour wall as one by one the marines took it in turns to stamp on his hands until he finally let go.

Tiny Little Silver Balls

When Paul went to prison, I cried at first. Not for Paul but for me. Then I started to behave strangely. Wild. Restless. I felt so alone, like nothing mattered at all. It seemed I had no friends – no one to talk to, no one to trust, nothing to share.

I would get drunk and write Paul really long mad letters – sometimes ten or twelve pages. Mum told me he had made a little box out of matchsticks to put them in. But he never replied. I didn't mind: it was like I was writing for both of us.

Paul, do you remember the mercury? We would sit at the top of the stairs – four flights, skinny and wooden – and we would roll the mercury out of the bottle. Tiny little silver balls, forming and re-forming. And us at the bottom of the final flight, ready with hands open to catch the tiny drops.

Looking back, I think we've always been lucky.

FATHERLAND

The Fortune Teller

Rochester Market, 1978

I watched her. She was a real showman, full of style. A large crowd of women stood around, clinging desperately to her last word.

'I'm not going to promise anything, but you have all seen me. You can all make your own minds up and if you're not satisfied, you keep your money. Just one object. That's all I need. I may tell you your past, your future, or things you never wanted to know. Just one personal object.'

She was thin and bony, about fifty, tall with dark brown skin, white hair and gold hoop earrings. Her hands were covered with brown freckles. Her knuckles looked large; they were split and protruding. Really bad arthritis, I thought, although she didn't show any sign of pain.

'You, young lady, you look eager to know something. Two pounds, and I may be able to tell you what you need to know.'

I passed her two pound notes with one of my earrings.

She held the earring tightly in her hand. 'Now remember, if you're not satisfied, your money will be returned.'

She raised her voice. 'Oh, ladies and gentlemen, this young lady has something special. She has a special kind of intelligence, not like yours or mine. What she has comes from birth, an intelligence thousands of years old.

'I see a dark man on a horse. He has black hair and black skin. On his head he wears a red hat, and he carries a sword by his side. A strange land. I see your ancestors mercilessly persecuted, running. I see mountains, red mountains. I see trees bearing the fruits of the gods. I see you walking wild, barren lands that hold nothing but dry red soil and thistles. You are on a snow-covered mountain and fierce winds are blowing.

'I tell you, ladies and gentlemen, this young lady is clever. Not clever like you and I. Her ancestors survived massacres. They are a shrewd nation.

'I see you on a boat, a rough sea-journey travelling from one strange land to another. I see your ancestors taking the same journey, but they are men descended of a race of giants and they have arms of steel. I see chains, but there is freedom at the end of these chains.

'I see a beautiful valley, green with orange groves, fed by

fresh water springs. I see sheep grazing on a hillside and a man making bricks from clay and straw, a primitive man by nature but, like you, he has this strange intelligence.

'I see you on a journey, an unexpected journey where many doors will open for you. Doors to your past, within which you will be able to live in freedom.'

She handed me back my earring, asking, 'Are you satisfied, madam?'

I wasn't. It didn't make a word of sense.

Looking at her, I said, 'No, but you take a pound for your time and I'll take a pound for mine.'

She handed me back a pound note and, smiling at the audience, said, 'You see, ladies and gentlemen? I told you she was intelligent.'

Getting to Know My Enemy:
In My Father's Words

'I was born in Cyprus. My parents were Turkish. My grandparents owned one of the last of the wine groves where they still made wine and other local drinks for their own table. They used to keep their wine over twenty years in vats: Commandaria, thick like honey and strong in vitamins.

'I do remember that whenever my mother became pregnant she used to send me on the back of the donkey with four large red clay pots to my grandmother's to fetch some of this wine. My mother used to take one glass of it daily, for health.

'When I was eleven years old, my mother became ill in the typhoid epidemic and within four days she had passed away. My father cancelled my scholarship for further education in Istanbul and university in the UK.

'I started work in a Turkish Delight factory, working from seven a.m. to seven p.m., and on Saturdays doing the gardening at the house of my employer. Part of my work was to take the daily shopping to his house and go back to pick up his lunch.

'The wife of my employer, she was so beautiful. They used to call her the Turkish Delight. But she was a bitch, a regal dictator. She was twenty-four years old. On Thursdays she usually lit the Turkish bath, purpose-built in the house, and she used to ask me to enter the Turkish bath and scrape her back. And she used to lie on the marble and let me massage her all over her body, and she used to wash me and she would do the same for me. Although I was only twelve and a half years old, I used to get the urge and she loved to play with me. Until I said, "This play must stop. If my boss finds out, he will cut my throat." She said, "He will never find out because you are my trusted little lover, and I will teach you how to make love." She then made love to me and took my virginity at the age of twelve and a half.

'Yes, she had two perfect legs, like a goddess, blonde hair and olive-coloured eyes, and her breast was pure white, like an angel's without wings. It was here that I took my first alcoholic drink, brandy, as we made love.

'With sex and hard work and not enough sleep, I was forced to give up my job and started as a house-boy in the British colonial administrator's house. Here, the social life and the British girls filled the day. They used to call me the

Elephant Boy, Sabu. I was soft and tender, making love to girls and women in the most passionate way, so that they would see stars in the sky at noon.

'I started drinking, socially at parties, but by twenty-four I had become a compulsive drinker and a compulsive lover. I gambled, I smoked. My body and health deteriorated as it became impossible to cope with too much sex, overdrinking, sleeplessness, gambling, and sixty cigarettes a day.

'By one-nine-six-two or 'six-three, I felt I had cirrhosis of the liver, beginning at my back passage. But in spite of all medical advice, I said that if I am to go today, I will die a happy man, with women around me and brandy in my hand.

'It was not until the first week in January, one-nine-six-three, that my best lady, Liz, told me she was pregnant. After four years of strong sex sessions with me, she had become pregnant.

'Yes, I was shaken by the news. Yet, still, I was saying to Liz, "Come on, have a child." She said, "Why?"

'I used to say, "Just to see if she or he will be as sexy as you." But Liz would reply, "Oh, no. God help us if the child takes after us."

'Well, He blessed us with twins: a boy and a girl.

'The result of this shock was that I prayed and prayed to God, the Supreme Power, to do something about my problems.

'I went to the alcohol unit first. As it happened, I drank twelve double Scotches, half an hour before I went into the hospital.

'The withdrawal symptoms were bad. After eight days, I

was allowed to walk in the snowy gardens of the hospital. Suddenly I came to realise that I was being cruel to my body. Why? Why am I doing this to me? I start questioning, asking myself:

'(1) Do I have to drink to be sexy?
(2) Do I have to smoke to be social?
(3) Do I have to gamble to make money?
(4) Do I have to be over-sexed?

'For the first time in my life, I realised the four above acts were my enemy.

'I left the hospital without permission and went out to find my enemy. I went into the bar where I'd had the twelve double whiskies. The bar attendant immediately poured a double, but I asked for a tomato juice. I went into eight bars and one restaurant. I had tomato soup, roast lamb and apple pie. For many, many years I had forgotten the taste of food. My God, the taste of roast lamb was so good. It stayed in my stomach when before nothing could stay in me.

'This walk round the bars, when I found the strength, despite the weakness of my body, to face my enemy, alcohol, and realise that I could give it up, in turn gave me the strength to return to the hospital. The specialist, when he saw me coming back sober, was shocked.

'The conclusion: whatever you do, do in moderation. Now, I enjoy good food and fast women but no alcohol, no gambling and no smoking. I hope to enjoy life and the gifts of life until I am ninety-nine years old.'

Going Home

We stood on the bridge. My father waved his hand over the sea. 'You see all this? You see all this, Tray? This is the same sea that your great-great-great-granddaddy sailed across two hundred years ago.'

Weird, I thought. Really fucking weird.

We were on a ship sailing from Turkey to Cyprus and a hell of a storm was brewing. People were still boarding the boat, carrying TVs, hifis, live chickens and boxes of oranges.

My dad went to sort out the cabin. 'It's going to be a rough crossing,' he said. 'We need a cabin in the centre of the ship.'

We arranged to meet in the bar. When I arrived, it was full – full of men with aeroplane collars, moustaches and hip-huggy trousers, smoking cigarettes. I went to the bar and asked for a whisky.

The barman screwed up his face. 'Whisky?'

'Yes,' I said, holding up one finger. 'One whisky.'

As he poured it, I looked around. At least a hundred pairs of eyes stared back at me. All men. I turned towards the bar and looked at my whisky as it slid up and down the bar top of its own accord.

I pulled out a cigarette and raised it to my mouth. Three flames suddenly appeared. I turned to the man on the right and took his light. As he babbled away in Turkish, he kept his eyes fixed firmly on my breasts. I said, 'I'm sorry. Please don't talk to me as I feel a little sick.'

His eyes lit up. He moved closer, nostrils flaring. He ran his tongue over his gold teeth and started to rub his groin.

I knocked back my whisky, picked up my cigarettes and box of matches and shouted, '*Defel. Gitorer.*' Get away. Fuck off. Conveniently, the only words of Turkish that my dad had taught me. There was a hubbub, and the men started to laugh.

My dad appeared suddenly from nowhere, looking like something out of *The Godfather*, with his pinstripe suit and dark-shaded glasses. 'Hey,' he said. 'Hey, Tray, what's all the fuss?'

I told him what had happened. My dad leaned in and whispered in my ear, 'Let's have some fun.'

When my dad had appeared, the man had shuffled half-way across the room. In Turkish, my father said to him, 'Do you know . . . do you know who I am? I am Enver Emin and this is my daughter. She may be drinking whisky, she may be smoking cigarettes, but she is no whore. Now, listen to me. On this voyage, if you say one more word to her, if you even look at her before you leave this ship, then I will have your bollocks cut off and have you eat them. And then I will have you thrown into the sea.'

As our ship made its way through the night, fighting through the tail end of a hurricane, my dad told story after story about his past and I chain-smoked.

As I lit another Turkish cigarette, my dad said, 'What's that writing on your matchbox?'

'I don't know,' I said. 'It's in Turkish.'

My dad took it, and as he read it, he started to laugh.

'What's it say, Daddy? What's it say?'

As he translated, we both screamed with laughter.

Meet me on the bridge – when your father has gone to sleep.
Ali

Under the Shadow of the Mountain

I woke up tired, not feeling good, two hours too early. I couldn't work out if it was the excitement of going, nerves, the sheer disappointment of being alone, or regret at having drunk so much wine – another bottle, four and a half glasses – to relieve the boredom.

It never seemed like much at the time, but in the morning it always felt like more: more of the same numbness. It never led to answers.

And M hadn't phoned or called by. So, I guess I was suffering from disappointment. I just lay there. I should get a curtain. If I got a curtain I would sleep longer: no light. But I had made myself promise not to live with any excess comforts. Could a curtain be considered a comfort? Was it good to sleep with so much light? But, then, I couldn't sleep.

I started to roll around and move a little. I had been doing this every morning for a while now; it went on for hours if I let it. I would wake too early, consider the curtain argument, think of M and start rolling.

I could hear the postman. I knew it was him – I could tell by the flap of each letterbox and his footsteps. All of a sudden, perhaps because of nerves, I had a feeling of dread: it was most probably a bill, a big fat rotten bill. Every box was going, one by one. He was on my floor: one, two, three. Me next – *bang* – drop. Same old sound. I lay there wondering what was at the foot of the door. Maybe a letter from M. I jumped up: fuck, the flat was hot. It was like a space capsule, no air, warm dry heat.

Picked the letters up.

Bank.

Telephone.

Council.

On the whole, not good. I sat at the table, the scene of the crime. Toy gun: unloaded. Bottle of wine: empty. Nine-page love letter: totally loaded. Oh, God, how had I got so carried away? Two Spot-the-Ball coupons covered with love hearts – not a winning attitude. I made some tea, ran a bath, thought about M long enough for the bath to go cold. Drank the tea, cooked some eggs, put some hot water in the bath. And so the morning went on, until suddenly I was late.

I never understood that timing. First, too early, then too late. Never an in-between time. The only time that is good is the time when the thing is happening.

I sat on the tube and started to count the stops: it would take forty-four minutes. I would get there by twelve forty-five, check in, no luggage. Then straight to the post office. I was feeling okay – a book open in my hand, reading; something I had found difficult. Since 1989, I hadn't finished one book. I had started, maybe a couple of hundred and some I had read almost to the end. Then I would put them down and never finish them. Mostly, I only got a third of the way through. Sometimes I think: I wonder what happened to Ridley Walker? Or, How did Byron die? Or, Would the sixth meditation answer all the questions of mankind? And so on. Reading was a hard one. I had picked four books for the journey and taken a bet with myself: they might be read but they would not be finished. Plus, the one in my hand was Russell's *History of Western Philosophy*: not a slim volume.

Terminal Four – next stop. I was an hour and a half late so at least there would be no queue at check-in.

Istanbul Airlines: two extremely long queues. In one, a million men with suits, moustaches, no ties, and trolleys loaded with suitcases full of electrical equipment. In the other, women, wife-folk, with headscarves, handbags, babies and grandmas. The whole thing depressed me. If I had been with someone else, I knew I could have been witty about just these sorts of things. But my head hurt, my hat was hot and people kept staring at me. I realised I looked odd, like I had the hat but all the other accessories were missing.

I handed over my ticket and passport. An Ankaress débu-tante said, 'Istanbul?'

'Yes,' I said, half yawning.

'Luggage?'

'No luggage.'

'Smoking or non-smoking?'

'Definitely non-smoking, and an aisle seat – I have a weak bladder. And *no* babies.'

She looked at me numbly.

'I don't want to sit next to any screaming babies, thank you.'

'I cannot help that,' she said. 'Most people have already checked in.'

'My point – if they have already checked in, you don't have to put me near them.' I smiled and walked off.

The post office was a challenge. The man in front of me had a letter that he insisted must arrive on Sunday. The clerk tried to explain, while I started to explode. Finally, I was served: three first-class stamps, please. All the rest of my post – all forty-four letters – had stamps. It was only M's two letters and the return to my bank that needed them. I put the letters into the box one by one. Usually I make a wish with such a large mail-out. It was my own sweet way of appearing *international*. People always behave out of character at airports. I usually play the part of a top model or a rock star's girlfriend. Once, I even bought a copy of *New Scientist*. But today I felt tired and pissed-off.

As the last of my letters went into the box, I heard my name being called over the Tannoy: 'Will Miss Emin please go to Airport Information?'

I panicked: somebody had died. No, too obvious. Perhaps

I had dropped my passport or maybe someone had come to see me off. I wasn't alone, after all! I would soon be thirty thousand feet up, but I would know I was not alone.

I rushed to Airport Information. A fattish woman sat there, giant bags under her eyes. 'Yes,' she said.

'My name's Tracey Emin. Did you just call out my name?'

She pressed a few buttons on her screen. The woman next to her smiled at me. She was on the phone. A call, I thought. Someone on the phone for me! I moved over to her and the first woman reared up: 'Excuse me, I'm dealing with you. Would you mind coming back?'

I moved back.

She stared at her screen. 'Yes, we did just call someone. A Miss Simmons.'

I sort of half smiled. 'Oh.'

She looked really annoyed. I felt self-conscious. 'Sorry, I must be cracking up.'

Someone was banging on the door. What door? My name was being called. Somebody said, 'Don't be frightened.'

'I'm not frightened,' I said. 'I was naked anyway.'

The whole house was banging. The tiger-pattern blanket lay across me. The light flickered and the tiny colour TV flickered, too, filling the pauses. Christ, though, the wind. It was smashing against the house. How could someone design a house with so many doors, so many shutters? But I was afraid: I had been dreaming something stupid and Freudian.

A.C. was looking out of the window. I was naked, quite

by chance. And I was explaining to him what the small ivory things were that stood on the railway platform. They were odd little things: some black and some white. They resembled the tiny hearts that I had drawn on my Spot-the-Ball coupons. Only here, in my dream, they looked irrelevant.

Me and A.C. walked back into our compartment, where everyone else was sitting. It was then that I realised I was naked. 'Oh, fuck,' I said as I tried to cover myself with a navy blue reefer jacket.

And there in the corner, someone Freudian was staring at me: only Lord fucking Byron.

I put the corkscrew back into the bottle. The time was ten thirty, by the clock opposite. I'd been having problems with the time all day because of the clocks in England. They had gone backwards – or forwards. The time in Cyprus was either one hour or two hours ahead, or behind, the old English time. Or the new English time. The whole experience had persuaded me to dispense with my watch. Strange things always happened when I did not wear a watch.

As a child, it had been impossible to wear a watch. I don't remember ever knowing the time. I remember learning to tell it, though it never made sense. Every day, one by one, we would all have to tell the time to the teacher. We would work it out, one at a time. Paul and I could never get the hang of it: we were always wrong. Well, not wrong exactly – just, never got it. Then, one day, we could do it. As twins, we often did things at the same time. We had our own language until we went to school, we were ambidextrous, telepathic . . .

Anyway, I suddenly had an urge to put my watch on. Time or no time, I wanted some worldly security. That's what watches do: they keep us bound to this world. Dreams don't have time. Neither does sleep, nor death. That's why it is sometimes good to wear a watch.

I always took my watch off when making love. Even if I kept all my clothes on. Even if it was outside in winter, I would always take my watch off.

Today had been so strange.

A few of us were driving in some kind of small bus, like a Dormobile. Someone said, 'Have we got the car?'

'Yes,' I said. 'It's stuck between the front wheels and the back.'

We passed fields, tall corn blowing. It looked very ghost-like. The road was straight, a clear pathway to a flat stone building, black flint, open slitted windows – medieval. We turned right at the building, past a windswept market-place. I wanted to buy something but we just kept moving. I didn't know the other people; well, I did in as much as I had always known them, but I couldn't tell who they were.

Down a sloping hill, on to a beach, along a cliff face, across wet sand and green moss-covered rocks until we could go no further.

The sea was coming in. I was worried. 'We've drowned,' I told them. 'We've come the wrong way. Please, we must go back!'

The wheels reversed, along the wet sand, up the hill and along the corn-lined road.

We stopped in front of a fake Victorian high street. I got out and walked into a pub with very low wooden beams. I was immediately given a drink and sat down at a long table opposite an old woman. She looked Freudian. I asked her where she had come from: could I know her from somewhere? She told me I was too young, she had been married in 'sixty-five.

'I was born in 'sixty-three,' I told her.

'No,' she said. 'Eighteen sixty-five.'

'But that makes you over a hundred.'

'Oh, no. I'm only eighty-two. And you're thirty.'

'No, I'm not. I'm twenty-nine!'

An old man next to her started laughing. They seemed harmless but I was confused. I was thinking of leaving when I found myself in an unknown kitchen surrounded by most of my family. Everyone seemed preoccupied. Mum was opening a very large deep freezer. Then the door opened and in walked my brother, Alan. I was so pleased to see him. He smiled at me. Then my uncle Colin followed. He looked strange: odd clothes – grey collarless shirt, very plain grey flannel trousers and a beige jacket. His hair was longish. And he wasn't walking – he kind of hovered towards me.

'Uncle Colin,' I cried, and went to kiss him. But something made me pull back. 'I can't kiss you,' I said. 'You know I mustn't kiss you. If I kiss you, I'll die.'

My uncle Colin smiled, such a kind, knowing smile. He reached down and said, 'Tray, it doesn't matter.' And kissed my lips.

Then he told me that nobody else knew I was there. Alan had a sense of me but I had to accept that life was over.

Daddy was sitting on the bed. The light was on.

'You slept with the light on.'

'I know, I know. I was afraid, I thought they'd come and get me.'

'Who?'

'I don't know. Oh, God, did I have a strange dream! I was in this pub. I had a drink and I was talking with these people at a table. And . . .'

'It doesn't sound strange to me.'

'No, listen. Uncle Colin was in it. He kissed me and we were both dead. You know, if Uncle Colin hadn't been killed, I'm sure our family would have been a lot different. Dad . . . Dad, are you listening? Did you hear what I said?'

'Yes, my sweetie-pie. I'm listening. I was thinking of my grandmother. She said, when we are born so, too, is a porter born. A porter of death.'

I said, 'I suppose we're all born to die. I sometimes – well, a lot of times – wish that I had never been born. I'm convinced I arrived here by mistake. I know it doesn't make sense but I really feel that if it weren't for Paul I would never have been born. I could have stayed where I was.'

'And where was that?' Dad said.

'I don't know, but I wouldn't be me. And I wouldn't be here.'

'Then tell me, sweetie-pie, what would you be?'

'Dad, it's seven o'clock in the morning. Can we drink our tea and plan the day?'

'I thought you would like to pick olives.'

We carried the wooden ladder up the hill, with two buckets.

'There's a secret,' said my father. 'We get a hundred pounds for every four sacks. And it only takes a day for three of us to pick one sack.'

'Dad, are you sure about this?'

He looked mischievous. And excited. I remembered all the olive stories he'd told me: the season was like a village war.

The hillside was rocky, a little difficult to climb. I knew we looked funny: the ladder and the buckets were difficult to handle.

We found our tree.

Dad placed the ladder against a spindly branch. It all looked very hazardous. His brown, bear-like body trundled up, bucket in hand. I stayed on the ground.

It was amazing – hundreds and hundreds of olives.

The bucket sat on the ground and he ran both hands along the branches, then cupped a handful of green olives. It felt therapeutic. Dad was miles away, as though a thousand feet up in the air. He looked almost god-like, perched on the branch of the tree with the olives, the blue sky and the mountains. I imagined what he must have been like as a little boy. I wondered if he had ever been much of a little boy: his mum died when he was eleven. He only went to school for two years and he was seduced at the age of twelve by an Englishwoman of forty.

I got tired of picking so I lay down for a while. More village people arrived to pick olives. There were a lot of jokes going around – general olive-talk. By noon, it was time to go back to the house.

I carried the buckets with the olives and Dad carried the ladder. As we crossed the road, a car drove past slowly. A woman peered through the window with a look of disgust on her face.

'Olive thief!' I screamed at my father.

His eyes closed and a big smile spread across his face. We both staggered about laughing.

'They're God's olives,' he said.

'You don't believe in God.'

'No,' he said. 'But that woman in the car does.'

We were both laughing. We knew we looked suspicious: it was the cameras and the sunglasses, we felt, that had given the game away.

As we came towards the house, he said, 'Tray, now I know you're not big-headed. Okay, you won't get big-headed. But, above all, you – of all of them – you are my favourite.'

My father had ten children altogether – ten that I knew of. And, as far as I was aware, we had no secrets about that.

Tuesday: just stayed in bed all day. Sleep with no sleep. Thought with no thought. Love with no love.

Everything felt distant, separated from me. I even tried masturbating but it went wrong – my mind wandered off. When you have the fantasy you're not quite sure what's going to happen in the end, but then you find yourself having a warped conversation from six months ago – the way you wished you had had it. Then you are in a library, reading a huge book on the occult and the last thing on your mind is sex. Even with yourself.

I got up. My watch said one fifteen; fuck knows what that meant. Maybe twelve fifteen. Maybe two fifteen. Maybe three fifteen. Maybe eleven fifteen. Maybe I shouldn't have bothered.

The sky was cloudy. Strips of cumulus; not puffy, slightly grey, with blue next to them. The house was under the shadow of a mountain, the mountain stretched down to the sea. As the sun set, it rolled along the summit like a giant ball down steps. At the third step, at seven o'clock, it disappeared.

I said to my dad, 'What happens after step three?'

'There's no sun,' he said.

I looked across the valley. 'There's sun over there.'

'Well,' he said, 'go over there.'

'No, that's not what I mean. I mean, if there's no sun here, how come there's sun over there? And why isn't it dark here?'

My dad just raised his eyebrows. 'Where is the sun?'

'Behind there,' I said.

He just smiled.

Just keep running. The hill is steep. I'm sure I'll fall. Just run. Keep moving and don't stop. Soon I will forget. It's hot. I can't breathe. My heart hurts. I haven't run for fifteen years. I can feel the ground through my feet.

Every part of me feels alive.

And now the sun is on my neck. Burning, every muscle throbbing. An explosion of blood and oxygen flies around my body, over which I have no control.

I had no control.

I just screamed at him, 'You can't – you are *not* going to marry her and that's that.'

'Why?' he said.

'Because – because it's disgusting,' I said. 'You must be mad.'

'And you,' he shouted back, pointing his finger at me, 'you are my daughter, my little girl. My favourite. You are the one I love, the one I trust, the one I would give the world to. The one who always, always, understands me.

'You are the one whose life I do not question. The one who always does what she wants, and learns in the only way she can . . . I never question you.' He slammed the door, shouting, 'But I have had enough. Where are you? Because I can't get through to you.'

I picked at my dinner. Loads of oil ran down my chin. Tears sprang in my eyes. As though on cue, great sobs heaved from my chest. For ten, fifteen minutes, great heaving sighs, gulps and tears.

I made a cup of tea, put it on the tray with his favourite biscuits and knocked on his door. 'Daddy, I've made you some tea.'

I pushed the door open. Like a wounded bear, he was curled up on his bed, his paws covering his hurt brown face. I put the tea down and more tears streamed. The gulps, the cries.

'Shut up crying, you stupid girl. Toughen up. You don't

cry, not in front of me. Pull yourself together. Stop crying now – stop it.'

I stopped crying.

'Now, what's really wrong?' he said.

'I fucking hate that woman and all her bloody peasant family. And I don't want them here any more. And you can marry who you fucking like, but don't expect my approval. I know that's why you brought me here, to see what I thought. Like when I was a little girl, you'd take me to offices and business lunches and ask me what I thought of this person or that person.

'And I'm telling you, I don't like this woman. And I don't trust her. I didn't trust her from the moment she said the olive tree was too crowded.

'And another thing, all this olive business. From four a.m. to seven p.m., olive, olive, olive. I thought we were supposed to be on holiday together.

'And I hate the fucking kid that runs and screams all over the bloody place. It needs a good slap.

'And I hate her bloody smoking, and I hate the way she eats. It's repulsive, the way she spits out her olive stones all over the place. *Pow. Pow.*

'And the way she dresses – she's a fucking peasant.

'AND YOU NEVER MARRIED MY MUM, SO WHY THE FUCK MARRY THAT OLD HAG?'

'Well, you shut up,' he screamed. 'Shut up, shut up, shut up! You got it wrong. I'm not marrying her! I'm marrying her daughter.'

*   *   *

I did my calculations, sixteen, thirty-two, forty-eight, sixty-four, with nine years left over – father, grandfather, great-grandfather . . .

He was old enough to be her great-grandfather . . . father, grandfather, great-grandfather . . .

Sweat was running off me as my feet pounded the ground. I must be moving very fast. Faster than I've moved for years. I wonder if I move faster when I'm dancing. But that's in one place: it's a motion-free action, in a single spot. Running is directed. I know I want to get to the bottom.

The light was blinding.

'Here you are,' he said. 'And I brought you these. I picked them myself. And I cracked them myself.'

He handed me five fresh almonds. I half smiled. My eyes felt like puffballs, swollen and sore. And not mine. It felt like I was seeing the world through someone else's eyes.

'You know, Tray,' he said, 'I'm surprised at you. I thought you would be more liberal.'

'Liberal?' I yelped. 'I've never been liberal about anything.'

'No, no. I don't mean liberal. I mean bigger. I thought you would even find it funny. I know your sense of humour, Tray. You laugh at life. You used to be able to see the other side. *I thought you would understand the game.*'

'I do, Daddy. But it doesn't make sense. I know what you're doing, I can see why. But I don't trust it. She's sixteen, Daddy. You're seventy-three. What happens in ten years' time when you're too old to fuck and she's out there, or even in your own house, with someone else?'

'Well, Tray, if that happens, it happens. But for now I need someone to cook, look after the house, wash my clothes and keep me company.'

'But, Dad, I think it's wrong. And the reason I don't like her mother is because her mother's a pimp. She's selling her daughter to you, and what for?'

A gigantic smile spread across his face – big white teeth. 'You know me well,' he said, 'but you will always be my daughter.'

It was *hot*. There was a haze over the sea. I sat on the terrace. Huge sheets were covered with olives, laid out to dry. A carpet of gold. The white sheets were staining where the olives lay. It looked beautiful.

He came out. 'You want your eggs fried?'

I sort of nodded.

He was happy, singing, doing little dances. He wore his purple shorts, a short-sleeved shirt, open, and a straw hat.

Today, I thought, he's really someone.

He came out holding the frying-pan. 'Tray, are these done enough for you?' Three eggs floated around in a vast quantity of oil.

'I don't think I can eat them,' I said. 'They're disgusting, *fatty* – and I don't like eggs fried in olive oil.'

'Okay,' he said. 'I'll eat them.'

He dished them up, and put one on to my plate. We sat there in silence, and ate.

'What are you thinking?' he said after breakfast.

'Not much.'

'Go on, tell me, Tray. What's on your mind?'

'Nothing really, Dad. I was just thinking what a great egg that was.'

Clouds swung round the top of the mountain. It all looked so beautiful. And my dad, he – he looked like a king among it all. He stretched out in the chair, his head facing the sun, a big smile across his face.

'What are you smiling for, Daddy?'

'Oh, I was just thinking about Queen Victoria.'

'What about her?'

'You know when she owned all the colonies? The British Empire. Well, sometimes she would go out and visit her lands. This time it was to be Jamaica. The royal ship set out from London, a long voyage. On board was every kind of provision, every kind of luxury.

'One day, Queen Victoria was bored so she summoned the ship's cook. She told the cook, "I want you to make me the most beautiful cake, something splendid and magnificent. And then I wish you to present it to the most beautiful child on board ship."

'The cook went off with her instructions and set to work on the cake. It took two days to complete and it really was magnificent. The cook sent a memo to the Queen that the cake was finished. A few days passed, and the Queen's curiosity got the better of her. She sent a note to the quarters of her son, the little Prince Albert, to ask him how he had found the cake. The child's nanny was confused by this. She went to visit the Queen to ask her what cake she was talking about.

'The cook was summoned and an explanation was sought. "Why did Prince Albert not receive his cake?" demanded the Queen. "Well, Your Majesty," replied the cook, "you never told me it was for Prince Albert."

'The Queen said, "Yes, I did." "No, Your Majesty," replied the cook. "You told me to give the cake to the most beautiful child on board the ship. So, of course, I gave it to my own son."'

I was smiling.

'You know, Tray,' he said, 'how Queen Victoria was given Cyprus?'

'Yes, Dad. You've told me tons of times. She spent one night in Istanbul at the Sultan's palace, and the next morning she boarded her ship for England, carrying the title deeds of Cyprus with her.'

'Good,' he said. 'You remember. But do you know what the young Princess Elizabeth said after she married the Greek Philip? She was very young, sweet and inexperienced. But beautiful. Philip, he was different: a real man, full of Mediterranean passion. On their wedding night, he took the princess in his arms and made passionate love to her. In the morning the princess awoke and said, "Philip, oh, Philip. That was wonderful! Do you think the poor people have it, too?"'

'No, Dad. I didn't know that.'

We were laughing. He had started on his Queen jokes.

'The English,' he said. 'They have some good points.'

'My mum's English,' I reminded him.

'Yes,' he said, laughing. 'That's what I mean. The English have good women.'

And off he went, Mr Olive, with the bucket and the ladder. Waving, he said, 'I'll be on that tree, over there.'

I lay there, stretched out star-shaped, my face squashed against the pillow. Oh, Christ. Oh, God. Oh, fucking hell.

This should be paradise. I should be in heaven. I should feel *love*. As I stared into the darkness, the corners of the room receded until they were a thousand metres away. My mind began to revolve around the space, spinning and turning. My heart was screaming, M – why the fuck don't you phone?

'Got to get to M. Got to get to M.'

I stood on the edge of the bed. The air was cool. I couldn't see anything. I stretched out my arms and jumped. First I went the wrong way, my arms started to ache. I thought of turning back but didn't know how to. All I knew was that I had to get to a place of love. I felt the continents pass beneath me. Sometimes my body was vertical. At others I flew like a bird, flapping my arms up and down. I sensed that I must look silly. I knew I was wearing a bright turquoise sleeveless top.

England was green and hilly, bathed in Prussian blue light. An unreal landscape with small terraced houses.

Ohh. My body was shaking. I was hot, my head felt as though it had been pressed between two large slabs of stone.

Daylight – air – sun streamed through the french windows. Tears ran down my face.

Dad was standing there, 'Tray, I've called you three times now. Come on, my princess.'

He sat on the edge of the bed with a cup of tea and a plate of biscuits. I sat up and tried to take the cup but I was shaking.

'What's wrong?' he asked.

'I'm depressed. I can't get up. It feels like the end of the world. Everything's in darkness. The world's a great rolling ball of shit and I'm stuck to it.' I threw the covers over my head and cried, 'Leave me alone. Please, leave me alone. Please, Daddy. Just leave me.'

I heard him leave the room quickly and quietly.

I just lay there, the blood moving slowly around my body. Was I really all alive – no part of me had died? My soul existed, but outside me. Dear God, I thought, every part of me is bleeding.

It was a warm spring day. The sky was a Mediterranean blue and thin white clouds striped it. I rested my head on my arms. I was a five-year-old child again, trying to make sense of everything. Where had the mountains with the snow-covered peaks gone? Where were the fir trees that lined the valley? Why was the sea now hard and green when before it was a beautiful blue with giant fish and soft, lapping waves? And the stars, where were they? Why had night-time become so dark? Where had my beautiful world gone? We had been uprooted to the English seaside, to a giant warren of floors and rooms and corridors: Hotel International.

Strange living. I have always had a strange life. Never knowing what was true, living in a world of dreams. Christ,

I told myself, I've got to get up. But with the weight of my thoughts, I felt like I couldn't breathe. Why did I keep taking on all of this – this shit and keep feeling it even after it had passed through me a hundred million times?

They Never Get Jealous

'Do you know that your grandfather had four wives?' my dad said. 'He was black, the darkest man the island had ever known. They wouldn't let him marry your grandmother, so one day he came down from the mountains on his black horse and stole her from the village square. Of course, she was his first wife: my mother. She died in the typhoid epidemic of 1932 when I was eleven.'

'So he was married three times after your mum? What happened to the other wives?'

'He kept one in the village, one in the hills, the other in the mountain pastures. Oh, the plains of Cyprus, such beautiful mountains with fresh-water streams and—'

'All right, all right,' I said. 'But tell me, why didn't the wives get jealous?'

'The goats graze wild in the hills. When the sun sets, oh, such beautiful sunsets! The valleys, every fruit, giant fruits. The melons. Oh, the orange groves! The orange blossoms blowing in the breeze and—'

'Yes, I know, Dad. You've told me a million times. But tell me why the women, the wives, didn't get jealous. I mean, they must have.'

'Oh, no. Not of each other,' he said. 'They helped each other. Your grandfather had land, sheep, crops, orchards. One wife would help with the land, another with the children – so many children – the other would cook and clean. They would each take it in turns. Oh, no. Good Turkish women don't get jealous.'

'Your wife does. Your wife gets jealous of my mum.'

'That's different,' he said. 'I'm not married to your mother.'

A Conversation with My Father

'Dad, why didn't you marry Mum?'

'Because I was married to Sherafet.'

'It's a pretty name, Sherafet. What does it mean?'

'It means, "God look after you. Good health."'

'Do you still love her?'

'Yes. In a responsible way.'

'Why did you marry her?'

'Well, I was in my early twenties, maybe twenty-two, twenty-three. I was doing my national service at the time, and my numerous duties took me all over the island. The name of Enver Emin became notorious from one end of the island to the other. I was noted as a drunkard, a womaniser and a black.'

'What do you mean, *black*?'

'Well, your great-great-great-grandfather was a slave in the Ottoman Empire, back in the late eighteenth century. He came from Africa, the Sudan. It is said that he had the body of a giant, and that he gained his freedom by slaying a whole army of Christians single-handed. I'm sure that cannot be true. Regardless, he was sent to the island of Cyprus to live a free life and raise a family. Very few African slaves survived. Even if they did, the chances of them raising a family were very low, because the Sultan ordered that slaves were to be castrated. The majority of Turks are fair – it is only the sun that turns our skin olive. But my skin is somewhat darker because of my great-grandfather and his father.'

'Yes, but what about Sherafet?'

'If you wait a minute, I'm coming to that. Each time I had my leave in the army, I would go back to my home village. It's very small, about two miles outside Nicosia on the south side of the island, a beautiful Greek village, high up in the hills with plenty of water and good land, which means good crops. Turks and Greeks would live side by side like brothers.'

'Tell me how you married Sherafet.'

'It was my usual leave. All the men of my village were sitting on the porch, drinking blindly, when my second cousin started to boast of his upcoming proposal of marriage to Sherafet. He had good reason to boast: he was forty-two years old, eighteen stone, stood five foot five and had the manners of a pig. I had known Sherafet since the day she was born. Her family worked the land next to ours. She never wore lipstick or fancy dresses like the other girls. But

103

no matter how plainly she dressed, to me her prettiness always shone through. She was like a little sister to me.

'I couldn't stand the thought of that fat animal with her so, in my drunkenness, I ran to her family's home. Sherafet's mother answered the door. She had always had a soft spot for me, and even though she could tell I was drunk, she let me in. Once inside, I insisted on seeing Sherafet.'

'And then what happened?'

'Sherafet came, and I asked her if she knew what her family intended. She stood there like a little girl, looking down towards the floor. Her mother said, "Of course she knows. She also knows that it's what the family wants. The arrangements have been made. There is nothing she can do."

'I looked at Sherafet, her slender young body, her sad face. I knew then that I would marry her.'

'But what about her family, weren't they opposed to it? What did her father say?'

'At first, he refused. But, slowly, he changed his mind Our families talked and it was agreed that we should be engaged for a year. During this time, I would be watched like a hawk. My every movement would be reported to Sherafet's father.'

'What did your father say?'

'Well, he knew me better than most. He said I'd had mothers, daughters, French, English, Greek, Turkish brunettes, redheads and blondes. Now this sweet young girl was to be my wife, and that, wife or no wife, I would still be the same man.

'A year later, on our wedding day, according to tradition, my father had to give Sherafet lifelong advice. The people from our village sat in silence, all eyes concentrated on Sherafet. My father called to her, and asked her to be seated. She was still just fifteen, so young and frail, sat up high by my father. He said, "This is the advice I give to you, my child, on your marriage to my son:

"Draw yourself a cross.
In one quarter you will have a dry desert.
In another, you will have a fierce ocean with great waves.
In another, you will have a mountain with jagged rocks as
    sharp as swords.
In the last, you will have eternal fire, burning with the
    flames of hell.
Now go and throw yourself at any one.
This is the advice I give to you."

'And that is why I never married your mother.'

Cleopatra's Gate

Ismile met us at Adna airport at dusk. The rains had started early: it had been pouring for two days and the roads were under a foot of water. Ismile carried me to the car. He told us that the riverbanks were sure to burst. I wasn't interested. I didn't care if we were swept to oblivion by a tidal wave. I had been up since four thirty that morning, and all I wanted was sleep.

As we drove, rain pelted against the window. It would be a good hour before we reached Mersin, maybe more, depending on visibility. But Ismile drove hard and fast, like a blind man, into the night.

As I stretched out on the back seat, I thought about my

mother. Fifteen years earlier, she and Ismile had been lovers. They had run from Europe to Asia, pursued by my father and the police. They came to rest at the town of Mersin, where they lived among the squalor, slums and poverty until the earthquake. Hundreds of people died, hundreds more went missing; buildings, bridges and roads became dust. The authorities came and checklists were made of the survivors, so Ismile sent my mother to the safety of the surrounding mountains.

Finally, with my father's persistent searching, she was found. She had spent weeks up in the hills, living in a barn with goat-herds and peasants. My father persuaded her to return to England and she never saw Ismile again.

During the chase from Europe to Asia, my father and Ismile had crossed each other's path on more than one occasion – apparently they tried to kill each other at every opportunity. Now they sat side by side, like father and son. With this comforting thought, I closed my eyes and slept.

I felt my body lurch forward. The car had stopped. 'Are we there?' I asked.

'No,' said my father. 'We've stopped because Ismile wants to show you something important.'

Ismile raised his hand to the front windscreen. 'Look, Tracey. Cleopatra's Gate!'

I looked between their shoulders, with sleep-ridden eyes, and concentrated beyond the screen, but all I could see was blue-darkness, rain and the constant back and forth of the wipers. 'Oh,' I said.

They both looked at me, a little disappointed. I suppose

I was meant to be impressed. As we drove away, I asked, 'Why is it called Cleopatra's Gate, then?'

My father answered with a bemused look. 'Because this was where Cleopatra crossed from Asia to Europe.'

I looked back, focusing through the dark, trying to get a glimpse, but thinking of my mother.

BLONDE ATTRACTIVE MILLIONAIRESS DISAPPEARS WITH HER YOUNG TURKISH CHAUFFEUR.

News of the World, 10 November 1969

Old Women

My dad was singing. I opened one eye. The village lights looked like giant stars surrounded by the darkness of the mountains. I closed my eyes. I could feel we were descending. My dad drove slowly round the mountain bends into the night . . .

She was calling me, a hunched old woman. I couldn't see her face, but I was sure she had a million wrinkles. I raised myself from the seat. My legs and arms felt stiff, as though I had no real control over them and could not put my feet down. She beckoned me with her hand: a dark old woman. I was sure she had no eyes.

I moved awkwardly through the air and, before long, came

to a giant stone door. It opened, and in front of me lay a spiral of steps. The old woman was gone. Down and down I went to a greater blackness. I could no longer see: the darkness had taken over. I reached the bottom, where my feet walked across fresh soil. Though I could see no colour, the smell of the soil told me that it was good red earth, the colour of the sun.

Music, strange music: drums, tambourines, flutes. Where was it all coming from? Four old women came out of the darkness, dancing. They made a circle, moving like young girls, as though they had been given a partial gift of youth. Toothless and smiling, their hands touched my shoulder. Round and round they took me. The red soil became dust, the dust became air, the air became nothing and we were floating. I tried to scream but my mouth wouldn't open. My screams were only alive in my mind.

His hand was on my forehead. 'My little darling,' said my dad. 'What a dream. You were screaming.'

My face was covered with sweat, and my words were jumbled. 'Dad, Dad, they pulled me through. Four wrinkled old women, dancing round and round. They took me somewhere.'

'They weren't old women,' said my dad. 'They were angels, angels of this earth. The Prophet Muhammad said old women never go straight to heaven. Just before they reach heaven, they are made young and beautiful again.'

The Washing-day Argument

As we drove from the sea, the land became a rolling mass of drunken hills. My eyes fixed upon the setting sun, a giant orange ball resting on the thin line of the sky. As I watched it melt away, the sky was streaked with a million bands of gold. My father smiled at me. 'What are you thinking?' he said.

'All that sun, all that gold,' I asked him, 'how does it move? Where's it all going to?'

He smiled and said, 'That giant ball of fire that we call the sun stays just where it is. Didn't you know that it is we who move round it. It is we who are constantly leaving.'

*　　　*　　　*

I woke with a jolt. My dad was shaking me, 'Wake up, wake up, you silly girl, you were dreaming again.'

The mountain sun streamed into my eyes; a bright white light pierced through to the back of my mind. I closed my eyes again.

'Come on, don't go to sleep. We are already there.'

'Where?'

'In Kastamonu,' he replied.

I looked out of the window. Everything was covered with a blanket of snow. Small rooftops started to appear. I rubbed the sleep out of my eyes and, in the early morning, our old village began to make sense. I opened the map: a small dot, high in the Ilgaz mountains, somewhere between Ankara and the Black Sea.

Women walked past in the snow, their necks stooped from carrying heavy water pails.

'You see up there?' said my dad. 'Up that wandering, goat-neck hill, there is a spring of boiling water from the centre of the earth. That one spring keeps the whole village supplied.'

Four or five women sat round a tap. They were beating clothes on a slab of marble. Hot steam rose and the soap suds ran into the snow. They sat hunched, kneading each garment as though it were bread.

Out of the car it was cold. God, it was cold. As we walked, the snow snapped under our feet and the crisp air filled our lungs. My dad started to smile, his dark brown face against the snow with big white teeth. 'You see the old wooden house on the hill? That's where you lived with your mother. Do you remember?' he asked.

'Of course I do,' I told him.

Pointing to the veranda that ran all the way around the house, he said, 'That's where old woman Sufi chased you with a large pair of scissors. She was going to cut off your hair and sell it at the market. Do you remember?'

'Yes, Dad,' I said. 'I remember.'

Getting excited, he said, 'You see the hollow behind the house? Well, do you remember when the rains came and flooded the village? I made you a small boat out of an old barrel and you sailed it over that piece of hollow land. And how about when you cried because the other children threw stones at the donkey – you must remember that?'

Yawning, 'Yes, Dad, I remember.'

Now he said, 'You see those two poles with the line across? That's where your mother used to hang her washing.'

'Christ, Dad,' I said. 'How incredibly interesting.'

He looked a little hurt. 'You mean, you remember so much but you don't remember what happened to your mother's washing?'

'No, Dad, I don't. Come on, tell me.'

'Well,' he started, 'your mother had washed her smalls and hung them on the line – brassières, white panties, her stockings. Now, you know how Turkish women dress.'

I looked across the road to the four or five women. They were big and fat, covered from head to foot: big black bloomers, dresses over dresses, shawls and headscarves.

'Now,' he said, 'twenty years ago all the women in this village still wore the yashmak to hide their faces. You know your grandmother in Cyprus—'

'Yes, Dad, I know all about my grandmother and how she tore off her yashmak in front of the whole village because she wasn't allowed to marry my granddad. But what about Mum's washing?'

'Well, as you know, Turkish men and women live different hours of the day. They go to the mosque at different times. There is a different place for the women to sit – they don't even use the same seats as the men. And, you know, if they are bleeding, they are not allowed to enter the mosque.'

'Yes, yes, all right, Dad. Just tell me what happened.'

'Anyway,' he continued, 'the women go out early in the morning, the men from midday until late at night. One day, the head woman of the village had to run an important errand. She passed by our house in the mid-afternoon and saw your mother's washing. Within ten minutes, all the women from the village had gathered together. Your mother and I were on the veranda, and we saw them marching in a mass up the hill. Outside the house, they called to your mother and demanded that she take her washing down.

'Your mother, being typically English, didn't understand the way of the Turkish women. She just laughed. The head woman shouted, "You tease our men, you make them hungry. They will leave us village women and go to the towns and cities because you tease them. They will go in search of city women who wear underclothes like those you have hung for all to see."

'By now, your mother could not stop laughing. I told her to go and take the washing down but it was too late. The village women tore down the line and your mother's white washing fell to the ground.

'We watched from the balcony as fifty fat Turkish women, covered from head to toe, trampled each garment into the mud.

'But, of course, that was twenty years ago,' he finished. 'A lot has changed since then.'

'The yashmak isn't worn any more,' I said. 'I suppose that's a start.'

'Yes,' grumbled my dad. 'Fat, ugly faces.'

Atatürk and the Hats

The district of Kastamonu lies 150 miles north of Ankara. Here, in Kastamonu, was our village. At one time it had been very small, with maybe ten or fifteen families, but many of the nomadic tribes from the east had settled there. The people were hardy, strong and basic. The majority still lived in the traditional way. Many had never gone further than the surrounding villages. Money was of little use, barter being the main method of trade. The village was self-sufficient.

My dad had found the old villa, with its ramshackle veranda, where I had lived as a little girl. There was an old woman leaning against it. She looked about a hundred and I wondered if she might remember me.

As we approached the house, two police officers strode towards us. They were large men with big coats, flat hats, guns slung round their fat stomachs. 'What are you doing?' one asked my father.

'Just looking around.'

'You are a Turk?' asked the policeman.

'Yes,' said my father. 'By birth I am from Cyprus. This is my daughter. She is English.'

'Do you carry a Turkish passport?' they asked.

'No,' replied my father. 'I am a British citizen.'

'But still,' said the policeman, 'you have the blood of a Turk in your veins, and so does your daughter. I am afraid you will have to come to the police station.'

My father and I didn't ask questions. You don't when two men are holding guns.

The police station was an old building. The Turkish flag hung outside. Inside, it smelt musty and all the furniture was pre-war, made of dark oak. We handed over our passports and wrote our names in a big black book.

A policeman searched my father, and then we were asked to step into the captain's office. A fat man sat behind a big old desk, and behind him was the biggest picture of Atatürk I had ever seen. Fifty smaller ones, covering the entire wall, surrounded it. Atatürk with his car. Atatürk at the 1923 Paris Conference. Atatürk in colour. Atatürk in sepia. Atatürk opening a hospital . . .

We sat down. On the captain's desk there was a picture of a woman with two small children and next to that, a photo of – yes – Atatürk.

'What seems to be the problem?' asked my father.

The captain smiled. His mouth held more gold than the gold market. 'It's your hat, sir.'

'*My hat?*'

I looked at my dad's hat: lamb fur, Russian-looking with a crease in the crown. It rested on the side of his head.

'Sir,' said the captain, 'you are a Turkish man. You have the blood of a Turk. You know the Turkish law. You know of the great Atatürk, the man who transformed Turkey from a third-world peasant land into a thriving modern nation. Yet you walk openly wearing the hat of the old Turkish way. Do you support the old Turkish way? Do you openly abuse all that Atatürk has done for our country and our people?'

'Forgive me, Captain, for I am a foolish man. It is not my intention to dishonour the great Atatürk, but I have been in Britain since one-nine-four-eight. I wear the hat to protect my head from the cold. I am an old man and my hair is thin.'

My father took off his hat. The captain smiled. As he returned our passports, he wished us a pleasant journey. We all shook hands.

It was cold outside. My father put one arm tightly through mine, his hat tucked securely under the other.

'Dad,' I said, 'it's bloody freezing. Put your hat back on.'

'Hmmm,' he grumbled. 'Did I ever tell you about Atatürk and the Paris Conference?'

'No, Dad. But you told me how Queen Victoria earned the island of Cyprus. She spent one night at the Sultan's palace and the next morning she left with the deeds of Cyprus.'

'That's right,' laughed my father. 'But this is a different story. Well,' he cleared his throat, 'when Atatürk came to power his main aim was to modernise Turkey. The Turks had for so long been seen as barbarous peasants. They had never been regarded as European. In 1923, Atatürk was invited to a great conference to settle the scars of the First World War. It was to be held in Paris and all the European leaders would be there. Atatürk was one. Now, Paris is the city of style. There would be press, newspapers, film. Atatürk wore a fez, the traditional Turkish hat. The fez was dyed henna red; it still is. Every man who wore the fez, carried a red line across his forehead, Atatürk included. He could not go to Paris in the headwear of an ignorant man, so he ordered a trilby hat from Paris, grey with a black band. He arrived at the Paris Conference in style: the modern Turkish man.

'Photographs arrived in Turkey of Atatürk as the modern man. His government knew that this was the new way. It was symbolic – a contradiction of the sultans and the old ways. Before Atatürk arrived back in Turkey, his government ordered five hundred trilby hats from Paris.

'Now, the fez was often ill-worn as it was generally made only in one size. Atatürk's ministers thought the same of the trilby. Upon Atatürk's arrival back in Ankara, he walked from his train to be met by a five-hundred-strong welcoming party, standing in rows on the platform. Turkish men with short back and sides, black leather shoes and grey flannel suits. But to Atatürk's dismay, on top of these smart Turkish men sat five hundred extremely badly fitting trilbies.'

The House of Mevlana the Poet

It was five thirty a.m. The lands of Konya lay covered in a thick blanket of snow. I was tired: I had travelled non-stop for twenty-four hours, and now I sat outside the house of Mevlana. As light came, men started to arrive. They all looked at me curiously.

'We do not open until nine,' said one.

'I know,' I replied, and told him I was happy to wait: I had come this far.

At eight o'clock I went inside the courtyard. The snow had been cleared away and below my feet were beautiful tiled patterns. From tiredness, I could hardly stand. I sat on the edge of the courtyard fountain and took off my shoes and socks. It was so cold – this was a fountain of ice water – but I washed my feet, arms, face, eyes and ears, nose and mouth. I covered my hair with a small scarf and entered the museum. On the doors was written:

Come. Come whoever you are, an unbeliever or a fire-
  worshipper,
Our covenant is not one of despair.
Even if you have broken your vows a hundred times
Come, come again.

Once I was inside, I was overwhelmed by the most beautiful music coming from everywhere. Tears ran from my eyes. Between my tiredness and the tears, I could see old men sitting on long boxes, playing flutes with their heads bowed low. I bowed my head, too, and looked at the floor. I thought, I must not disturb them. I raised my head slowly for one more glimpse, but they were gone. All that remained were beautiful covered tombs and at the end of each there was a name, a date and a turban.

I knelt on the floor with my head pressed to the ground and said my prayers:

'Dear God, in this life there is no innocence,
And this we all should know,
For when we do not, the guilt is unbearable.

When we do not know,
We learn to live with it.

On this earth, there is no return,
No great salvation.
Some may say they find it in wine,
Other in the turning of the tide,
But for those who do wrong
There is no rest.'

Strange Land

This is a love story – a True Love story – of the deep and burning passion between me and a man old enough to be my father: a Turkish man, a fisherman, a mountain man. It was wrong for us to be lovers. His wife became ill, his children unhappy. He let the apples rot on his tree. He spent his days making me tapes and writing love letters. He spent the family's money developing the photographs we had taken and telephoning England long-distance.

At the airport, his big hands pressed against the glass. As I looked back, he was crying. I never saw him again.

The last thing he ever said to me was, 'Make our story beautiful.'

I yearn for a lover who wreaks havoc by rampages,
Whose heart burns, who drinks and spills blood – who defies
the stars,
Wages war against heaven, whose fire – even when it takes
a plunge
Into the bottom of the vast sea – still flames and rages.

Mevlana

Abdullah was forty-five, a fisherman from a small village on the south coast of Turkey. He was married, and had been for twenty years. He and his wife Sekra had four children, the oldest eighteen, the youngest three. Sekra had had six abortions. *Why?* I asked Abdullah He said that the doctor at the hospital had told him that if she had any more children she might die. But now the doctor said the operations themselves were dangerous. Abdullah did not want Sekra to die so the doctor had sold him some pills. They would stop her getting pregnant, but she was very ill. Her eyes were tired, her cheekbones rose high, and when she walked, she held her head low. Abdullah had told her to walk like this; in fact, he told her to do everything.

When Abdullah knew that our love was possible, he told Sekra that she must either sleep with cotton-wool in her ears or go up into the White Mountains. Sekra fled to the mountains, taking their little son and daughter. She told her friends in the village by the sea that it was cooler in the mountains. This was the beginning of summer.

For four months, Abdullah and I were lovers. We spent

our days drinking Izmir red wine. At night we would go out on the small boat and fuck like crazy in the sea. We would climb up hills and sit on top of Lycean tombs. He would play the *zuz* and I would dance. We were like performing bears – performing for each other. It seemed to be just us and the sea; there was no right and wrong, just mad, blind love.

When my father announced he was coming to the village, people told me, 'Be careful. Your father is a Turk, a Turkish father. He will shoot Abdullah and drag you away.'

My father drove his car into the town square. He did not come with my mother, or with his wife, but with his other woman. He was sixty-eight years old. The other woman was thirty-five. Their daughter was six. I had never seen my little sister before; she was beautiful, with dark brown curly hair, and, like me, she loved our father. When I saw him, I knew he was afraid: afraid that I would be jealous, afraid of the sadness I might feel for my mother. But he had no reason to worry. My own fears were far greater. I had prayed a thousand times on the night before he arrived: 'Please, God, I beg you with all my heart, please let Dad understand. Dear God, I ask just this one thing.'

My father drove the three of us into the White Mountains, up to the village where we had been told Abdullah's wife lived in a small, white stone house. She lay ill with grief; she lay waiting for her husband to come to her.

Our visit coincided with the annual market. Hundreds of tents had been pitched. The air was thick with the smell of sheep and goats, the streets were packed with cattle, the stalls filled with pots and pans, wedding dresses, all in chaos, all for sale. Abdullah held my hand tight, saying, 'This way.' Everywhere we went he greeted his relatives: this was a village where everyone knew everyone, and each shared the blood of someone else.

Abdullah and my father bought meat, bread and vegetables. We entered Sekra's house. She lay curled up in a ball, water streaming from her eyes. As she raised herself, my father asked her what was wrong. She said she had been ill for five days: heavy diarrhoea, bad sickness, pains in her back and stomach. My father gave her some tablets. She cooked a meal, She cooked enough to feed thousands. Villagers kept looking through the doorway; children peeped through the windows. In the heat of the kitchen, I saw grease running down Abdullah's face and, for a moment, I hated him.

Sekra smiled and thanked my father for the tablets. Abdullah said goodbye to her and we made the return journey to the village by the sea. The next day, my father left for England. But before he went, he told me to tell Abdullah to go back to his wife, just for a few days. He said that Abdullah must look after his apple trees: the crop would be ready soon. And he must pay more attention to his ox and his donkey – they looked sick. And he must chop wood for Sekra to makes fires, as the evenings were cold in the mountains.

In our nights on the beach, we would make a small house out of seven umbrella stands and a giant piece of white sailcloth that Sekra had sewn together with tiny little stitches.

Inside, we would lay mattresses and cushions. To me it seemed like a miniature harem tent. Before I was ever with Abdullah – and before Sekra had been sent to the mountains – I would watch as, night after night, the two of them made their own little house. I had loved it then, and even now I wonder if it was perhaps this little sailcloth house that I had wanted so much. The house that Abdullah and I built together each night. We would joke in Turkish that we were becoming married – 'evlenmek', literally 'to make house'. Before Islam, before Christianity, to marry was simply 'to make house'.

Once built, the house stood three yards from the sea. As we slept, the waves would turn. In Turkey, there is no tide, just the forward and backward throw of the waves.

Even after the sun went down, the nights were hot and sticky. The flies were in love with me: they loved me like I was a piece of donkey shit. One night I counted over sixty bites. They drove me insane. I would wake up tearing my skin to shreds. On these nights, Abdullah would douse me with paraffin. One day, he found the local doctor and asked him why the flies bit me so. He told the doctor that he was afraid the flies would send me away. The man laughed and told him my blood was sweet.

Some nights, we would go to the town. Between the sea and the town lay a large hill, so we always travelled by water, sailing in Abdullah's tiny fishing-boat. There are no flies at sea. In the town, we would drink and dance, drink and drink until our drunkenness told us that it was time to sleep. Abdullah would steer the boat, singing happily about the stars, as I lay staring up at the moon. That journey, maybe we made it a hundred times, a thousand times, I don't know. Now and then there would be no moon: it would slumber between two giant mountains and the bay would be black, the sea blacker still. On one of these nights, Abdullah turned off the engine as the little boat approached land. Just as he was about to secure a rope round a rock, he looked at me, but I was gone. I had disappeared beneath the water. I had not screamed or cried but, somehow, slowly, quietly and drunkenly, I had slipped off the edge of the boat. Down and down, I went. The water was not cold, just black like a giant envelope covering me. It felt safe and I began to sleep, my mind filled with nothing.

He carried me from the water. I was breathing. I might have died, believing the sea was a warm bed. I would have slept if it was not for Abdullah.

After that, Abdullah became afraid of the boat, afraid of the sea, afraid of the wine we drank and the flies that tormented me. He asked God why I was being taken from him.

One night, when he had gone to take a shit behind the rocks, Abdullah slipped and banged his knee. Each day, his knee was more swollen. Then the morning came when he could no longer walk. Usually we would wake at daybreak when the sun first appeared and run into the sea. The water would be ice-cold. Streams of sweet water ran underground for miles from the mountains, finally pouring into the salt of the sea. Abdullah would submerge himself completely, three times, and say his prayers.

But on that morning, Abdullah rested on the rocks and asked God why he could no longer walk.

The nearest hospital was a four-hour bus ride away. On the journey, Abdullah began to cry in pain and everyone stared at us. Every ten minutes he would drink from his bottle of Cognac, which he said helped relieve the pain. An old man rose to his feet and shouted to the driver to stop the bus. He held prayer beads in one hand and the Qur'an in the other. He said, 'In the name of Allah, I demand that you stop this bus and remove that man. He is drinking alcohol. He sits next to a young girl while his wife and children go hungry. May God punish you all if you do not stop this bus.'

The driver would not throw us off, so the old man left the bus, as did five or six other townspeople.

At the hospital, hundreds of women were waiting with yellow, sickly-looking children. One woman said her baby was dying. The corridors were full of people, some moaning, some wailing, some crying. Young, old, they just waited. There was only one doctor. Abdullah asked me for ten thousand lire and passed it to one of the guards. The guard passed it to the doctor and we were seen straight away. The doctor smoked Marlboro cigarettes and drank tea, surrounded by ancient X-ray equipment.

I went to the toilet. It stank. There was shit and dirt everywhere. The whole hospital stank: everything was dirty and old. I was grateful that I wasn't ill, and thanked God for giving me good health.

The doctor did not know what was wrong with Abdullah's leg.

It was evening when we returned to the small town by the sea. Abdullah's fishing-boat lay waiting for us and, above it, on the harbour walls, people sat talking. When a taxi drove at us from across the quayside, all we saw were the headlights, coming straight for us. Abdullah pushed me out of the way and shouted at the driver, 'You bastard, leave us alone.'

The taxi driver screamed back, 'Your wife is waiting for you.'

On the beach stood Sekra: a small figure on the rocks, looking out to sea.

Abdullah's sons helped him out of the fishing-boat. The sailcloth house had already been built, and washing hung on the bushes to dry. Sekra had arrived that afternoon. Someone had gone to the mountain village and told her that Abdullah was ill, that he had been rushed to hospital, that he might be dying, that his leg was going to be chopped off and he was calling for her.

Abdullah hit her round the head. He beat her with the back of his hand. He told her not to believe what other people said. He told her not to believe in village gossip and that she must sleep alone in the small house that night. Abdullah insisted that we would sleep on the fishing-boat.

As we went further out to sea, Sekra's cries became fainter.

I woke up. The sea was lapping against the side of the boat, a crescent moon hung above us, as though on a string, and a million stars lit up the sky. I asked myself, Why are the stars always closer in Turkey? I reached up my hand to touch them. I looked at Abdullah: his face was like a burnt old wooden spoon, his hands covered with callouses. He woke and asked me what I was looking at.

'The stars and the moon,' I told him.

He laughed. 'So you think I keep the moon and the stars in the palm of my hand?'

I pointed to the thin sliver of the moon, and tears ran down my face as I told him, 'When that moon is full, I shall be gone.'

Dreamhouse

In truth, it's a small cardboard house I made in my hotel room in Istanbul. The walls are from a cardboard box, the furniture from various things – the bed is a Marlboro packet, the bath a hotel miniature soap box.

I live in a tiny flat in London. I live alone. I have lived there for ten years. It's not homely. It's not particularly comfortable. It's always in a mess. At times, it's dirty: the times when it really should be cleaned, I call it home.

But I dream of exercising my taste. I dream of living somewhere with space. Often in my life, when I have really wanted something, I've made it up. Like, it's all I've thought about, dreamed of, craved and believed. And then it has become reality.

I carried my little cardboard-box house from Istanbul to London. It was so fragile that I was afraid it would get squashed. Mistreated.

I told the stewardess on the plane that it belonged to my daughter. Maybe one day it will.

TRACEYLAND

M*A*S*C*U*L*I*N*I*T*Y

M

Masculinity, Manhood. What makes a man a Man? As a woman at the dawn of mid-life, I can confess to having learned, for sure, that I have more testosterone in my right foot than most men have surging around their entire bodies.

You don't have to be born with balls to have balls. There is spunk and there is mental spunk, and it's the latter that gets me up in the mornings, that makes me change my life, that moves the world round.

As a child, I had the misfortune to be sexually abused. As a teenage girl of thirteen and fourteen, I fell into the ridiculous habit of having sexual relations with men much older than myself.

The truth is, these men weren't men. They were weak human beings, striving to redeem their masculine selves by fucking a thirteen-year-old girl.

A man should never think with his dick, and as he gets older, he should have learned to control the direction in which his spunk flies. Mental as well as physical. There is nothing more unattractive than a man who is sexually weak.

A

Anal sex, good old Victorian contraception. I believe it's still illegal in Britain between men and women. Not that you ever see the anal police sniffing and banging at anyone's door.

I was in a relationship once, some years ago now, when for three years I was never kissed, never held. Not only was I mentally abused, but almost every night I was subjected to anal sex. This was the closest I got to any kind of physical affection. I was split apart, busted up inside, suffered constant diarrhoea, piles and one infection after another. The so-called man I was having a relationship with based his life on the films of Martin Scorsese and Francis Ford Coppola, books by Ernest Hemingway and Charles Bukowski. He would stand in front of the mirror doing De Niro impressions: 'You talking to me?'

He never talked to me. But he bored me with a ceaseless diatribe of macho bullshit loosely based around generic rock-and-roll lyrics. He had an unhealthy penchant for young girls. I was nineteen, nihilistic and anorexic. Above all, I was incredibly weak and stupid to put up with him.

To take advantage of another human being, someone who is already a victim, whether male or female, is the biggest turn-off of all.

S

Size – well, it does matter. Tits, bum, crack, arse, mouth, dick: we all need a good fit. Especially when we're curled up at night, asleep. It has to feel good, or it just doesn't work.

There is, definitely, something to be said for the man who walks with a swagger in his pants. But why?

Women hit their sexual peak just before menopause. It's a well-known fact. But it is less well known that the female hole changes shape: in fact, it becomes tighter, smaller and harder to make wet. The defence system goes up.

But the man you've been married to for the past twenty-five years, the man with the beautiful big dick, the man who loves you, who has given you maybe one, two, three children, is confused and pissed off because his old ways no longer work. Will he have the confidence to stay? Or will he drift off to some slap-happy hole? It's not always easy being a man with a big dick. But it is definitely most attractive.

C

Charisma. This is something a real man has: history, presence, kudos. Someone who has something that most people don't. You can't touch it but you can feel it.

When I was at school, we girls all had a big conversation about what kind of women we would like to be. I don't remember what I said, but my friend Niki Calvart wanted to be the kind of woman for whom, when she walked into a room, heads slowly turned and then, quickly, a whisper bubbled round as everyone asked the same question: 'Who's that woman? Who is she?'

If a woman is young and very beautiful, this may happen. But a man can be fifty, sixty, eighty, grey-haired, quite fat, and it may still happen. And after the whisper has died down, the final word will be: 'I knew he had to be somebody.'

The idea of being with a man who is as good and interesting at eighty as he was at twenty-eight, whether he can get it up or not, is exceptionally fine.

U

Unfaithful. Men have a massive problem. They lie.

Here is a generalisation: the majority of men would be unfaithful, unless they were put under threat. 'Oh, my God, we're going to have a baby and I won't be the most important person in her life any more.' Or, 'My wife has become really boring, I want to spice up my sex life.' Or, 'I'm a failure in every way. But not with that really sexy stupid twenty-year-old. She boosts my ego.'

Why the hell would anyone be unfaithful unless they had fallen out of love? Twenty minutes, one night, it makes no difference. I have a female friend who is constantly unfaithful. I say to her: 'Why do you think you gain experience from other lays when the man you are with is not given the chance to grow?'

Being a man is taking responsibility for an action, whether it's calculated or just a fuck-up. Do not deny those you love.

L

Love. It's a hard thing. But I have always said, 'Just replace the word "Love" with "God" and the world will be a much better place.'

I

Intercourse. Once I'd got my head sorted out, when I was thirty, I had this strange and romantic idea that I wouldn't fuck anyone unless I loved them. Maybe it was because I'd had so many shit relationships, and two abortions.

I made a solemn promise to myself that I would only have sex if the person (especially men) felt really good. It was also at this time that I decided I didn't want to have sex with women any more. I always met women that I would either like as good friends, or if not, I would feel that I was using the women in a gratuitous or abusive situation, as a man might.

I would rather masturbate any day than break someone's heart.

N

No. No means no, no. And 'please' does not necessarily mean 'Please, fuck me.' It can mean 'Please stop', but there is no breath left to finish the sentence.

I remember when I was fourteen, crying on some sofa. I had just been fucked by an almost complete stranger. I mean, I knew his surname. He wasn't a bad person, but he said, 'Why didn't you stop me if you didn't want me to?'

I can count the times I have had sex – or made love – lying on my back. It has always been my choice to bury my face in the pillow. Sometimes I open my eyes and look over my shoulder. But these days, when I do, I smile.

I

I is for me. I cannot believe how much I have fucked up in love. At least, physically. I don't believe I have mentally. For some weird reason, all of my tiny horrors have been liveable. I have not died. In fact, life has become better. Through age and experience there has come realisation: life is worth living.

T

Telephone. There is always a way to communicate. Or T could be for Tracey. For years I was ashamed of my name. Tracey was synonymous with 'stupid'. But I'm not, and I've changed that.

Y

You know and I know what does and does not make a man. I always loved *Gulliver's Travels*. A giant man in a tiny world, a tiny man in a giant world. And there is one line I remember, though perhaps I imagined it: 'I like a tiny man with a lot of spunk in him.'

Well, I'm a tiny man and so have I. And I can prove it.

Remember, St Valentine Loves You

14 February 1988

I woke up feeling alone, so lonely. The night before, I had cried myself to sleep. I lay there on the floor, listening to the tube trains passing beneath me. I thought, All those hundreds and thousands and millions of people. *London, London – I hate you.* I picked myself up and got ready.

I missed Rochester: my flat, my cats, Maria, the table, the teapot, the river, the bridge, my pub, my walk along the Medway. The Valentine's Day post arrived and I sifted through it. Nothing there for me – *no love*. No one loved me. I started to cry.

I put on my Hush Puppies and picked up my umbrella.

It was a beautiful crystal day. The sky was blue, sharp white rays shone down, and I thought, Why do the lonely people stare up to the sky?

I got to college. Another traumatic day. But the bright sun still shone. The nights were drawing out. As I left the building people said, 'Hey, Tracey, why the umbrella?'

Sulkily, I said, 'It stops me feeling alone.'

On my way to Camden I sat on the tube, big tears welling in my eyes. I looked at the people carrying flowers, holding arms, cuddling and kissing. I felt so fucking lonely that the tears ran down my face.

I left the train at Euston and hobbled along the platform, trying to find my connecting line. It was like a maze and I was lost. I couldn't see where I was going because my eyes were still full of tears. I went up some stairs and along a winding tunnel. I heard a noise behind me and turned, sharp. A man.

A man wanking.

I looked in front: there was nothing, no one. I started to run, he grabbed me and held my arm, tried to pull me up some stairs.

I didn't look at him, just elbowed him with all my might and ran. But I was running in a maze: where were all the people, all those millions? I ran and ran. I jumped down some stairs, and found corridors to my left and right. *Fuck, which way should I go?* I could hear him, his heavy breath, right behind me. I turned back towards the stairs and as he stood there – a tiny, puny, ill-looking soul, grinding his teeth – I raised my umbrella like a golf club, held it high and, with a voice that sounded as though it came from hell, said, 'You come one step closer and I'm going to smash your balls to kingdom come.'

With that he turned and went the other way.

People appeared on the stairs, all making a fuss: 'Are you all right? Are you okay? Are you okay to travel?'

'*YES,*' I said. 'It's okay . . .

'. . . *I'M NOT ALONE.*'

The Proper Steps for Dealing
with an Unwanted Pregnancy

Always use a condom – carry them with you twenty-four hours a day.

If things go a bit rumpy-pumpy and the condom breaks, do not lie back and think of England. A modern-day old wives' tale recommends using Coca-Cola. If you have been shagging *al fresco*, roll on to your back and have your young man assist with a bottle of Evian. Then jump around on the spot for five minutes. This may be fun – though it will not work.

Go straight to the chemist and buy the morning-after pill.

It actually works up to seventy-two hours later. So, do not freak out if you are nowhere near a chemist, or if it is Saturday night. Also, call Talking Pages – they can give you the address of the nearest twenty-four-hour chemist.

When you take the pill, try to be calm and not too hungover. And eat something, as there may be side-effects. Also, you may be feeling physically fucked-over and not just fucked.

If, for some reason, you did not take the morning-after pill, and your period is one minute late, go to the chemist and buy *two* pregnancy tests – Boots do a very good deal. Do a test straight away, preferably first thing in the morning, and the second in the evening. That way you can be more sure of a true result, in the event that you have a hormone imbalance.

If the test shows positive, call a friend that you really trust – maybe your boyfriend – and discuss the pros and cons.

If you decide that a baby is impossible, call the Family Planning Clinic, the Brook Street Advisory Centre or anywhere that will advise on unwanted pregnancy. If you have an understanding GP, call them too.

Have a blood test and a pregnancy test to be 100 per cent sure that you are pregnant.

At this point, you could ask for a coil to be inserted. This is painful, but it will ensure that the pregnancy will go no further. (I'm not sure if it's legal, but I did it some years ago. True, I couldn't stand the idea of sex ever again, but it worked.)

Insist on having an abortion as soon as possible. If you

have the money, you can be treated within twenty-four hours. If you go through the National Health Service you may have to wait up to six weeks.

Do not keep your pregnancy a secret, as closely guarded as the Crown Jewels. You may need moral support before an abortion as you will feel shit, weak, maybe sick and afraid. Talk it through.

Go to the clinic with a friend, not just for the operation but also for a preliminary visit. Check that the place is clean and the staff are understanding.

Once a date is fixed for the termination, do not go out on a guilt-ridden drunken binge. Stay calm.

After the procedure you may feel euphoric with relief. Be careful: depression may follow. If you feel terribly ill, go back to the clinic immediately. Two per cent of terminations fail. If the evacuation was not complete, the consequences may be fatal.

After a termination, some women feel fine, almost as though nothing has happened. Others feel extremely weak. Make sure that you have nothing important to do for the following forty-eight hours, that you have food at home and somewhere comfortable to curl up. You will need some care and attention.

If you feel you made the wrong decision, or if you suffer from guilt, ask for counselling. Regret is natural, but will pass with time. There is, too, the possibility that you may take out some kind of guilt-aggression on your partner (if you have one).

There is always the possibility that the termination will

result in the end of your relationship, simply because you feel you have experienced something so utterly alone. This is why it is good to talk through beforehand the decision to terminate.

You may feel terribly broody and want to steal babies. And you stand a high chance of falling pregnant again immediately. So, maybe for a short period, like six months, go on the pill. Just make sure that you are given one that suits you.

Drink lots of rose-hip tea, eat beetroot and take iron pills. Red meat, too, if you aren't a veggie. But the best thing is Floradix, available in tablet or liquid form from all health shops.

Think positive. Concentrate on all the things you could not do if you had a baby.

Exercise.

Try not to get too out-of-your-head as some weird, deep-seated emotions might fly to the surface when you least expect them.

Beware of phantom pregnancies.

And, most important, if you decide to have a baby, don't listen to anyone. Just listen to your heart.

Looking For Him
(The Sweet Smell of Desire)

I seek a lover.
A lover who wreaks havoc with my heart,
a life within a life.

A lover to kiss the palms of my hands,
to whisper that I will never feel
pain again.

I will kiss the lids of his eyes.
In love with his smile,

I will mimic his laugh.

We will lie in our own silence
listening to the rain,
the noise of passing cars.

My cunt is wet with fear,
I know I will always feel pain.
Every part of my body is bleeding
a wound of desire.

I know it's safer to be
Alone with

The kiss you left behind –
The sweet smell of desire.

Abortion: How It Feels

I was nineteen. I had sex with someone I loved – someone I trusted – because they believed in *The Truth*.

Two months later, I found out I had contracted gonor-rhoea. I had had it for three months, nestled inside me, growing and spreading. The clinic gave me a heavy dose of antibiotics but they didn't work. Something kept gnawing away deep inside me. The hot burning pain drilled into me.

I was fucked.

And at the clinic, months later, as they peered down some stainless-steel instrument, as far as the wall of my uterus, they said, '*Hmm.* Looks like it's all cleared up.'

I focused on the photograph of Charles and Diana on the wall.

'When was the last time you had sex?' they asked.

'Last night.'

'Did you know your partner?'

'Of course,' I shouted, as they pulled out the stainless steel.

Then they told me I'd never be able to have children: the gonorrhoea had seen to that.

For years, I had sex: not so many partners but always intense. In a way I didn't care that I couldn't have children. I knew the pitfalls: family without family, being poor to keep the poor.

Eight years later, I went to my doctor and asked, 'Are you sure I can't get pregnant? *Are you sure?*'

'Why?' he asked.

'Because I feel better . . .' I said. 'More alive, more awake.'

He told me, 'I am ninety-nine point nine per cent sure you cannot have a baby, but if you have a steady partner we could run some tests on you.'

I had missed a period. Not the end of the world – it often happened. But, you know, the strange thing was I felt different. Like, I cared about myself: my toenails, my skin, my teeth, my diet. I could feel the tips of my hair, and the ends of my fingers tingled.

I went back to the doctor and had a pregnancy test. It was Easter and the blossom had begun to spring on the trees. I phoned the doctor for the result. I was told to come in and given the next available appointment.

A week later, the doctor – a good Christian, tall and lean – said smugly, 'You're looking rather expectant. Have you thought you might be pregnant?'

'No,' I said. 'Not when you told me it was ninety-nine point nine per-cent impossible for me to be pregnant. It would be a miracle.'

'Well,' he gleamed, 'congratulations. You are pregnant.'

I walked through Regent's Park; the blossom, pink and white, floated above me, and the clouds floated above the blossom, and heaven floated above the clouds. And with both my hands across my stomach, I said, 'Hello, tiny. Welcome to this world.'

The next few days made things clearer. If I had the child, it would be my responsibility. I was alone. I couldn't think straight. I knew I had only a week or so to make up my mind and if I made a mistake I would have to live with a lifetime of regret. It seemed so unfair. Everything – all my life, everything I'd ever fought against – I was now part of. I didn't want an unasked-for child, dependent on my love. I didn't want to be poor or held hostage by the unknown. I wanted to die, not live for ever through the unasked-for. And although the art of making love can bring life, true love was not there. I was alone.

I went back to the doctor and told him, 'I can't have it. I need an abortion.'

He had a fit.

He showed me the photo of his baby son. He told me how precious life was and what a wonderful mother I would make. Finally, he refused to sign the papers.

I told him I'd pay – I'd go somewhere and get it done. Two hundred, three hundred pounds was nothing compared to a lifetime of poverty. In the end, another doctor signed the papers.

I was given my date: 1 May.

I arrived at the hospital at nine o'clock, exhausted. My boyfriend was with me but I felt so alone. The night before had been full of dreams, hot sweats, feeling sick. Waking, crying, the tears streaming down my face.

I promise with all my heart I will always love you, and no one on this earth can say otherwise. I will always love you. ALWAYS, ALWAYS, ALWAYS love you.

The words went round and round and round in my mind and my body, until I knew they were no longer my words but something that had been carved into my heart.

And now my soul was crying.

It was a square waiting room. Ten or twelve women sat there. Some were quiet, casually reading magazines as though they were at the hairdresser's, others looking distraught and holding tight to their boyfriends' hands. A few stared blankly into space. I sat there thinking, This is not me: I am outside me. Only part of me is doing this, to survive.

A nurse called me to go through. I thought I felt my baby's heart jump. 'Now,' she said, 'take a seat. You have left it very late. You're well into your third month. Are you sure this is what you want to do?'

The me that was not me simply said, 'Yes.' But in my mind I had started screaming, 'No, no, no, no, please, no.' And I could hear my little baby, crying, 'I want you. Please don't send me back, I want you. I want to stay here in this world with you.'

Looking at the nurse, I said, 'Yes. Of course I'm sure. It would be impossible. I can't have a baby.'

She asked me a few more questions. I signed some more forms. And I went back into the waiting room. My boyfriend was there. He looked so sad. 'Is there anything I can get you?' he asked.

'Yes,' I felt like saying. 'Get me out of here. Get me out of this fucking nightmare.' But I didn't. I just sat down and waited. One by one the other women went through.

It was now one o'clock. I counted. Since I had arrived another seven or eight women had entered the waiting room.

Now it was my turn.

I got undressed, carefully putting my new yellow socks into my shoes and laying my clothes across the plastic chair. I put on the white gown. The nurse took the metal clip off my hair, scraped it up and put it into a tissue cap. I lay on the bed, which was wheeled along the corridor.

I was taken down into the basement. That was where they did it.

The nurse held my hand. I could smell death and I told her, 'I'm afraid.'

She patted my hand and told me it would be fine. But I was going to kill, to murder, to end a life: a life that I could have loved for ever.

Nothing made sense. The nurse removed my jewellery and my false teeth. Then the anaesthetist came over and I was asked to sign a consent form. As my hand scribbled 'T. K. Emin' I thought, That's not my hand.

The anaesthetist made a small hole in my vein. As I started to fade, I tried to say, 'I'm sorry.'

When I came round in the recovery room, I was crying uncontrollably and in terrible pain. Two hours later I hobbled out of hospital.

I still felt pregnant, as if there was something that wouldn't let go.

I became delirious. Then my body swelled and my face became puffy. I telephoned the doctor and said, 'I don't feel well. I'm in terrible pain and I smell strange.'

'What do you expect?' he snapped. 'You've just had an abortion. How do you think you should feel? Any more problems, call the hospital.'

After five days, I was so ill that I went back to the hospital. My friend Gail called a mini-cab and helped me get dressed. I put on my flowery shorts and top. I couldn't walk properly and had started to ramble. I felt a bit mad. I was trembling.

As I got into the cab I felt something slip out of me, down the side of my leg. I caught it with my hand and held it there. Amid the London traffic and the summer heat, I cradled the foetus – my dead baby – between my thigh and the palm of my hand, knowing it had never wanted to leave me.

Postscript

Five years later –
it still hurts.

But I know I did
The right thing.

Small Hands

It feels like a million years, and my guilt is pressing down hard on my shoulders. At night I dream of hands, small hands, pressing deep into my palms.

I rise from my pillow, coughing. My heart is beating uncontrollably. The guilt is suffocating.

And always, in my head, I hear a strange voice that does not belong to me:

The dead and dumb are one year old, one year old today.

I have never asked why, just accepted these strange words, knowing, always knowing, they did not belong to me.

And now I am alone, and I sleep with strange words, which are always inventing themselves.

And all the things I think, and all the things I believe, are making me cry.

Feeling Pregnant

I have never wanted children. Well, that's a lie. Sometimes I have, but usually only when I am pregnant. I've always preferred cats. The idea of going to visit someone's new baby is always a nightmare, but if it was a kitten I would be round there like a shot.

Each month, just before my period, I have this mini attack – a kind of mini freak-out – when I lie in bed unable to sleep, holding and clutching myself, repeating the same words: 'Fuck, what if I'm pregnant?'

'Fuck, what if I'm pregnant?'

The strange thing is, for the past two years my period has come late: perhaps two or three days late. So there is always a night when I lie in bed, counting off the days on my fingers as I try to work out how many there have been in the past month. Then I pull myself together, rationalize the situation, and think: 'I know, I will deal with it in the morning'.

The following day, I always wake feeling strangely sick and queasy. And really hungry: a desperate craving for toast and jam. Strange, because I never normally eat sweet things. I'll go to the kitchen and before I know it, I will have eaten a whole bag of raw baby spinach, a packet of mini-cheddars and drunk three glasses of cranberry juice.

'Is this normal?' I wonder. (God knows what else I might have eaten in those previous ten minutes.)

Then I stand in front of the mirror, my stomach bloated and my tits really hurting. And I feel different: not myself.

I put my fingers up inside me and feel a gritty dryness but still no blood.

I go to the chemist and buy a pregnancy test and hide it in the kitchen on the understanding that I will give the whole situation twenty-four hours. I spend the rest of the day doing what I have to do, with the utmost efficiency. Everything is meticulously calculated, I am utterly responsible. But every ten minutes or so, I say to myself, 'Chill out Trace, you can't be half pregnant. You can only be pregnant or not pregnant.'

When night comes, I chain-smoke like a moron. I smoke like I have never smoked before. At ten thirty p.m., I go to the off-license to buy more fags and a couple of bottles of wine. I come home and drink the wine and smoke the cigarettes. Then I go to bed and lie there wide awake, holding on to my womb.

I feel really terrible.

At about five o'clock in the morning, I will feel very strange: incredibly hungry, yet sick at the same time.

At eight thirty a.m., having spent the entire night tossing and turning, I get up and put the kettle on. And I make a mental list:

A. Phone the doctor.
B. Don't tell a soul.
C. Take out £350 and go to Harley Street, to a good clinic.
D. Insist on having it done, straight away: four days pregnant is not the same as four months.
E. ?
F. See if I can take that French pill, the one that gives you a natural miscarriage. If I can't get it in England, jump on a train to Paris.
G. Be calm, cool and hard, and know it is all for the best. Cutting the root makes the tree grow stronger.
H. Keep repeating these words, 'cutting the root makes the tree grow stronger'.
I. Phone a friend, a friend that I can trust, just in case I need help.
J. Do a pregnancy test.

I go to the bathroom, knowing that within three minutes my life might never be the same again. I feel alone and afraid, yet excited by the danger. The fear makes me feel alive: in fact, I'm so afraid that I can hardly piss.

Three minutes later, I am staggering down the stairs with

the phone in my hand. This is not looking so good: 999 are talking to me but I am incoherent. I fall down the last stair, looking at my phone but quite incapable of understanding the voice coming through it.

The burglar alarm goes off, ringing loud in my ears. I am being propelled along, very fast. A mask covers my face, and I am told to try to breathe. I hear people saying: 'We have no choice, call the next of kin, call the next of kin.'

Everyone is panicking. I open my eyes, or I try to: they are crispy and stuck together. I scream but nothing comes out of my mouth.

'Where's my baby?' I demand.

A nurse puts a needle into the top of my thigh, leaving me dreaming of something beautiful and tiny and peaceful, all wrapped up in a shrimp-pink cloth. A small thing, curled like a ball. A dead ball, seen through the sad haze of a nightmare.

And then I wake and feel the sun burning my legs. I reach for the suntan cream and re-adjust my sunglasses.

She is holding a blue and white ball and walking towards me. She throws down the ball and sits next to me, like a little damp seal under the shade of the parasol. I call her Tiny (I never call her by her real name).

And then *he* walks towards us, and he is carrying three coconuts with straws sticking out of the top. Tiny has never seen anything like it before, and we tell her it's monkey juice and that the only way to drink it is to become a tiny sea monkey.

She is laughing and we are smiling. The sand is golden

yellow, the sea a rolling blue. The sun is pelting down and we are happy in this imagined moment of time.

I look at the pregnancy test: it's negative. Of course it's negative. Of course I'm not pregnant.

I am relieved, relieved to know that at thirty-seven years of age, I am just a woman with a fucking good imagination.

Art for Me Is Like a Lover – Whose Love Alone Was Never Good Enough

At the beginning of 1992, I left art. It was a terrible break-up: all part of my emotional suicide, when I attempted to give up everything I loved that did not love me back.

It was a destructive time. But also a time of revelation. I was twenty-eight years old. I had spent seven years in and out of art college. I had a first-class degree in fine art and I had spent three years out of art school, struggling to make something beautiful, only to arrive at the tearful conclusion that I would never be a great artist. My life was too important to chop it into little pieces in the attempt to make art. That was why I had always failed.

So, by July 1992 I had returned from failure to concentrate on what I believed I was good at. Like a wounded bird, I began to rebuild myself, using the experience of failure as my foundation.

I knew I could be good at something, and to celebrate this, I sent out eighty letters: a subscription form, inviting people to invest ten pounds in my creative potential. For this, they would receive four letters: three official ones, and one marked personal. Within the first month, I received sixteen replies and soon I had forty subscribers.

Kiss Me, Kiss Me, Cover
My Body With Love

I finished my drink and said, 'Well, I've got to go now. You know, things to do.'

I passed the off-licence and a voice inside my head said, 'Don't drink, Tracey. Rest, sleep, be good to yourself.' So all I bought was a bottle of Orangina.

I opened the door to my flat. It hit me: first the stench, and then the heat. Fuck, the first true day of spring and I had left the heating on. I took off my clothes and threw them on to the floor with the dust and dirt: eight weeks of never-ending shit, constantly increasing. There were piles of dirty washing, heaps of letters, opened and unopened. I stamped my way across the floor, through tapes, CDs, wine bottles and half-empty teacups . . .

The bathroom: every surface filled with used cotton-wool buds, dirty underwear, discarded pill packets, bits of old soap, a speckling of black public hairs and a yellow stain.

To the kitchen. That just stank. I found a glass, washed it six or seven times, then squeezed yesterday's Indian take-away into a large white plastic bag, which was already full. I pushed it to one side: three days' worth of rubbish and I was still fucking living with it. I washed my hands: nothing to dry them on. I pulled a dirty T-shirt from the ever-growing mountain of sweaty, stinky clothes.

I poured the Orangina into the clean glass and drank half of it, then filled the glass to the brim with neat vodka and ice. One day, I thought, I'll get myself a fridge. A great big fucking fridge and I'll fill the whole damn thing with ice.

I sat on the floor next to the phone and dialled the first number that came into my head. An hour later, I was still there, drinking neat vodka with a full ashtray by my side.

Reluctantly, I put down the receiver. Drunk and spinning, I made my way to bed. My bed. It smelt . . . it smelt like, like . . .

I should have changed the sheets – but I kind of liked it.

I thought of a film I'd seen about mites: dust mites, the kind that eat skin flakes. The kind that would now be having a great party in my bed. A microcosmic world. And here I was, a giant; naked, drunk, alone. I lay there, clutching my vodka, taking in my own smell.

Then I was sleeping. And out of the darkness came Joshua. He was back, hovering above me: smiling and laughing and pointing down at me. His shirt was white and open, his chest was bare. And I was laughing with my hand raised, pointing back at him.

I shouted, 'Inkibus.'

'Suskibus,' he shouted back.

As my eyes opened I could still hear him laughing. But he had disappeared. He had become light. My eyes closed again and I slept.

It was morning. A piercing light shot to the back of my mind. I reached for the Nurofen and dry-swallowed four. It felt like every bone in my face had moved by at least an inch.

I put my hands on my tits and held the soft, warm fleshy things . . . that did not belong to me. In fact, no part of my body felt like it belonged to me. My stomach was soft and puffy, my clitoris smooth and flat. It all felt sad, so fucking sad.

It always creeps up on me unexpectedly: my body and how it makes me feel. Today, I thought. Today, six years ago, I was pregnant. Fuck me, I actually carried life.

I put my fingers inside myself: unbelievable, impossible, that life could come from there. It was dry and tight: it was incredible that it could stretch so much.

I reached for the Orangina bottle and pushed it up inside me as far as it would go. It hurt. I fell asleep.

The phone began ringing. I let it. The bottle was still up there. I removed it, looked down and saw that it was covered

171

with blood: my blood. It was Tuesday. My period had started. The blood went down the bottle a good few inches. I thought about babies: the size of their heads. Fuck, shit, I thought. They can be really big.

My mind stopped hurting.

The sun shone through the window.

I was happy for the light and, staring at the blood and the bottle, I jumped out of bed. Smiling, I said to myself, 'Dear God, dear God. Only ever let me give birth to my dreams.'

Food Is Not My Strong Point

Food is not my strong point. There is nothing more depressing than trailing round supermarkets, filling the basket with meals for one.

I hate cooking. Maybe that's because, most of the time, I detest eating.

But one cannot live on vodka alone. I have also found that the more I eat, the more I can drink. Before I hit town, it's essential that I eat something – so, it's a quick trip to the convenience store or the all-night garage for one box of fish fingers, sliced white bread and, of course, tomato sauce.

Throw four fish fingers under the grill. While I'm waiting for them to go golden brown, with little black singed bits, I like to knock back a pint of Nesquik, preferably strawberry flavour. Excellent for lining the stomach.

Butter the bread, then give it a thin layer of tomato sauce. Remove the fish fingers from the grill and mash them into the bread. There you have it: the classic fish-finger sandwich. It should be washed down with vodka and a can of Red Bull.

The classic fish-finger sandwich has a number of advantages:

(a) Easy to eat in the bath
(b) Full of vitamins
(c) Keeps you going for hours
(d) . . . and there's plenty left in the packet for that drunken late-night snack.

When Flying

I usually sit with earphones on, watching a terrible film – one that's supposed to be funny – engrossed and laughing like a lunatic.

Two hours later, I'm crying my eyes out to *My Best Friend's Wedding* – the same bloody film.

Flying is tough. But it's like someone said to me once: 'When you land, you have to wait for your soul to catch up.'

Cum Quietly or Not At All

I find it difficult to concentrate and impossible to relax. My mind is hyper, my body is taut. I'm frustrated and, at the age of thirty-three, I'm sick to death of turning myself on: the *Great Wank*, when you give yourself a really good going-over. The same old fantasies – the cowboys, the lesbians, the skinhead boys – like the loop of a film going round and round. The dry orgasm, everything held inside . . .

. . . the constant meetings, the film crews, the phone ringing, the appointments – until, finally, the one important thing can seem like an afterthought: *art*. The art of living and wanting, needing to feel whole.

Which was why the biggest kick of the last few weeks

was joining my local video shop. For two reasons: (1) I never go to the cinema; (2) I like to work while I'm watching TV.

I took out two films: *Killing Zoe* and *Reservoir Dogs*. I chose both because they were supposed to be violent. I thought they would help me release some of my fucked-up, pent-up energy. But what happened was unexpected.

Eric Stoltz lay with his arms behind his head, flat out on his back, his mouth in a half-smile. As he and his leading lady happily enjoyed a joint orgasm, I thought, Christ, I wish that was me.

He was Zed, the safe cracker, and he was good at his job. I thought, Yeah, I wouldn't half mind him having a crack at my safe. So controlled, yet so dangerous: what a way to make love . . . where would it all end? The Zed Generation: I'm on board for that. The climactic moment. I knew it was only a film but somehow I couldn't – and still cannot – get his face out of my mind. It was a new kind of love: my first screen crush. As a girl I did all the usual things, collected posters, wrote 'David Cassidy' on the sides of my plimsolls. But nothing like this – me and Eric meeting in LA, me and Eric having dinner together: we love swimming, the same books, long walks by the sea, holding hands as the waves crash around us. I managed to transform my bored desire into a total fantasy.

The only problem now: to masturbate or not? It felt far too sordid. Inanimate objects that once could do the trick no longer had that special place. I had closed up. There was no room any more. I don't know if it was my affection for Eric's character in the film – or maybe it was the film itself: mad, crazy, so much blood.

I can't share my life with a fantasy, but most relationships are built on just that. People often share parts of their lives together in a totally surreal way.

Me and my mum spend most of our time on the phone discussing *EastEnders*: Grant and Tiffany; the prospect of Sharon returning to the square, perhaps with Michelle Fowler, both with babies, both fathered by Grant; the happy irony of Michelle and Sharon being truly related. We all slip into these unreal worlds as a release from the daily drudgery.

That's why people wank. Not just for sexual gratification but to let their minds roam – to send their thoughts on an uncontrollable journey.

Strangely enough, you'll find the less sex a person has, the less they masturbate. I have a close friend who assures me she has only masturbated five times in her life. Of course, there is the theory that she doesn't have a vagina. Then again, I know for a fact that most of her daily life, including her work, is wrapped up in fantasy. Leaving her eyes crystal clear. Unlike mine: yes, I am extremely short-sighted. And, yes, I think I've been doing it since the age of nine. But now, thanks to Eric, my wanking days could be well and truly behind me.

Postscript

I never got round to watching *Reservoir Dogs*.

Would You Like to Make Love to Me?

I wake up thinking of your body. I wake up listening to your mind. This morning I woke up dreaming of kissing you. I was drunk and called you to say, 'I love you and I am still alive.'

Tomorrow, there is a Sex Show at Olympia (like the Boat Show, but it's Sex). Now, even though I worked in a sex shop for a brief while in my teens, I know very little about sex (for example, the Michael Hutchence thing: I guess he pulled the belt through the buckle and threaded it through the door thing and held on tight). Anyway, I thought it might be fun to go. And somewhat embarrassing. See me blush!

Call me if you don't want to push my head into the pillow tonight.

X

All I Wanted Was Your
Spunk Dry On My Face

I dream of being fucked; I mean, really hard. A hand on the back of my head pushing it deep into the pillow.

I am sick of all the wanking. Sick of my *tiny* mind. My *tiny* mind that's forever expanding, rolling from one fantasy to another:

The gun's at my head. I'm sitting on a chair. And as he comes in my face – BANG – there is nothing, just white space.

She is masturbating with the mop. I catch her red-handed but she doesn't stop. She just gets more excited.

She is kissing me, her mouth small and open. Her long red hair, crystal blue eyes: she is an Irish dream.

And those 1930s women with the big black underwear and the short stockings.

The cowboys. With really big cocks. Fucking each other. I watch his hands as they cling to the edge of the bar.

It is silent, not one single sound. As though I am invisible, and I have just stepped into another world.

I'm on a horse, moving really fast. Faster than I have ever moved before. The sky is desert blue. I'm wearing jeans, my usual black bra, no shirt. And on my feet, a really old pair of cowboy boots. My hair is quite long and it flies out behind me. I ride towards the sun, followed by a cloud of dust. And as I disappear into the horizon, I toss my head back, smiling and laughing.

I hear myself shouting:

'Yee-ha!'

From a Week of Hell

Friday

Woke up having sex – with a terrible hangover. Ran to the bathroom to throw up, shitting at the same time, holding on to the pan. Small white balls of foamy stuff cascading out of my mouth. My whole body shaking. My eyes about to burst, swearing to God I would never drink again.

I threw up nine more times during the day.

Saturday and Sunday

Spent the whole weekend in bed, depressed and trying to recover, with a throbbing tooth and scabs breaking out all over my chin.

Monday

Woke up with a horrendous toothache. Took fifty painkillers and dabbed on a ton of oil of cloves. Went to pick up my pills too late; and too late by two fucking hours for the morning-after pill. Had to be fitted with an IUD: a piece of copper wire wrapped around a plastic hook. Indescribable pain as it was pushed into the neck of my womb. Told it could be taken out in a week and I would not be pregnant.

Tuesday

Woke up sad. Went to St Thomas's Hospital for a lung scan and a chest medical. Was told I had emphysema. Kept a copy of my breathing test. It amused me, a drawing made of my own breath. Still felt terribly low, knowing that I could end up in an iron lung.

Wednesday

The pain in my mouth was unbearable. Went to the dentist. By now, the oil of cloves had burnt my gums. I had an abscess and a totally fucked tooth that had to be removed. The dentist gave me some antibiotics – and a cast of my own teeth.

Thursday

Couldn't believe it was only a week ago that I went out and had a good time.

I got There at 11.30 —

Very nervos.

About The prospects

of changing my life

For Ever —

To Find out my appointment
was For 10.30 —

I Just burst
out in Tears

Love Tracy

The skeless.

My Booze Heaven

The phone's ringing. My head's ringing. It's Wobbly (Gillian Wearing).

'Wotcher, Wobs,' I said. 'Congratulations on winning the twenty grand.'

She begins to relate her highlight of the night before. And even though she was dead chuffed to have won the Turner Prize, it was my *Rock Maiden Rides Out* TV appearance.

'But I wasn't on TV,' I say. 'Last night I fucked up big time. I missed out on five hundred quid. All I had to do was sit there and talk about "Is painting dead?" But I blew it to celebrate with you.'

Gillian insists I was there, live on Channel 4, pissed out

of my brains, my final remark: 'I want to be with my friends. I've got to phone my mum.'

'Very funny, Gillian, but you don't get me like that. What a wind-up!' I hold on to the phone – my brain's about to explode, but I'm laughing – and turn to the man lying next to me. 'Oi, Mat, wake up. Was I on TV last night?'

Grunts, 'No.'

'Hey, Gillian, get off the phone. My hangover's too bad. Just take your humour somewhere else.'

I close the call with her still insisting that it's all true.

I go back to sleep thinking, How wonderful that my friend has time to crack a joke, even at the height of her celebrations, in the wake of her success.

A few hours later, I'm sitting in a café in Shoreditch, drinking coffee and feeling slightly more alive. I open the *Guardian*.

Complete fucking horror.

It's me, wearing my Vivienne tan top with the accessory of a bloody-bandaged broken finger, pissed on television. And now it starts to come back. It wasn't someone's house: those comfy chairs, those strange people. It wasn't a dream. It was real. *It was me*.

I switch my mobile on. The electronic voice tells me I have twelve new messages. The first is from Angela Bulloch (another Turner Prize nominee), laughing. Just her voice, laughing.

Every bloody message is the same: all my mates, all of whom caught the Turner Prize coverage on video.

Radio 5 calls me. They want a quick interview. The Tate calls to reassure me that I have caused them no embarrassment: *I am an artist and that's the end of it*. My gallery is inundated with requests for me to appear on chat-shows.

My art's selling like hot cakes.

My mum calls to say, 'Thank you for remembering me, even though you were on the point of unconsciousness.' (She had seen it on the news.)

All the phones are ringing every few minutes. I can't cope. I'm embarrassed and confused. I don't understand. It's like remembering nothing from your childhood, being shown photos, being told events and, bit by bit, assembling a possibly false memory from these fragments.

Am I now the George Best of the art world? He was a bloody good footballer, world class. But what is he remembered for?

I still don't understand why I behaved as I did, drunk or not drunk. My broken finger, and the painkillers I'd taken for it, must have had something to do with it, although that's no excuse.

New York Diary

Thursday

Thinking about the last time I was here: New York isn't a place to be alone and in tears. In fact, it's phenomenally difficult, a hell of a city to cry alone in. I lost all control – I just kept hugging myself, rocking backwards and forwards crying the same words, 'Oh, God, what have I done so wrong?'

Now, six months later I was sitting in a bar on 23rd Street with Amy. We were pissed out of our brains and chatting to some guy called Jimmy, our voices getting louder and louder, talking about art and sounding phoney: meaning, *folly* and *funny*. It was one of those pissed-up conversations that go round and round. I was sitting behind the moving optics, looking like some bug in the reflection. Jimmy had come to the conclusion that I was Amy's bodyguard and had some kind of control over the situation. Me and Amy were attracting attention, 'Fuck who'd have thought life could be so good?' kind of attention, the stuff that can give you an amazing sense of well-being. It was now dark outside and we had been drinking since four in the afternoon. We had gone to the bar on the basis of just one beer, which suited me as I had been up all night drinking and fucking. I sat on my stool sipping whisky like a crash victim – internal injuries. I saw this film once called *The Inkibus* (I believe), a creature that served both men and women, fucking any hole it could get into. All the way through the film, women would be found fucked to death astride the toilet. I could relate to that.

Sometimes in life you fuck and you feel nothing: nothing except *I am never doing that again*. I like being fucked to the point of unconsciousness, when my mind doesn't function any more. I think about Jesus being nailed to the cross, and I realise that I am the cross, a giant crucifix and Jesus fucking me. I am not religious but there has got to be something going on. For me, Jesus was a hard-edged guy, crossing the desert. A terrorist, maybe of love, with his own army, Mary Magdalene at his side.

Me and Amy left the bar, on the understanding that we were international women. Amy was anxious to meet up with Rex, to get her nose in gear.

Rex was in the gallery, as cool as ever, surrounded by a half-made model village, a large TV set and enough stimulants to keep a bloody army going. Mini the Mental was also there. Although I had felt ready for another binge, I collapsed on the gallery floor in my new cowboy boots and Missoni dress. I just lay with a beer in my hand unable to move. I was thinking about our ferry trip to Staten Island, sailing past the Statue of Liberty. From my new position on the floor, it all seemed so fucking unreal. Meanwhile, Amy was staggering around trying to find the loo. She eventually squatted over a glass and, for our entertainment, knocked back a large swig of her own piss with the words, 'Not bad. Warm, but not bad at all.'

Rex got me back to the hotel somehow and we spent the rest of the night in the bath. Well set up with fags, vodka and everything else on tap.

Friday

Woke up pissed. We went down Canal Street then I spent the rest of the day making a thatched roof. Guy the hairdresser turned up: he had made a tiny model graveyard. We all agreed how good we were, helping Rex to make his model village. We had to wonder why we didn't make them more often, rather than getting really pissed, taking tons of drugs and staying out all night. We could all have been master builders.

Saturday

A dull hangover and too much to do: I met Mini the Mental, Hamish and Karen at the gallery where I would be holding a show in May. Mini had come to deliver a blanket she found in the street. The night before, drunk, she had carried it ten blocks, only to wake in the morning and discover it stank. An 'Emin ready-made', as she put it. We all went for a few drinks. It was supposed to be lunch, but somehow vodka was the main dish. Mini suggested I patch a pair of cowboy boots on to the blanket. Hamish decided I should call it *Psyko Slut*. Me and Mini spent the rest of the day shopping, the last purchase being a litre bottle of vodka.

Got back to the hotel to find Rex had collapsed on the bed. We ordered some room service and started on the vodka. I filled as many of the tiny empty bottles from the mini bar as I could and put them in my little furry handbag. We got to the gallery about seven thirty. It was quite a shock that Rex had got all his work finished, considering the drink, drugs, fucking and general hair benders. I left Rex's show and went round to Amy's show. The main comment about her work was that she smoked too much. As far as I was concerned, it was a major coup: my two favourite artists were opening in New York on the same night and had fucking excellent shows.

The party was one big blur. It was at the point in the evening when the bar stools were empty that me and Rex lost everyone. We decided to go back to the hotel to get more vodka. Sadie rang us to say that everyone was in hell and we returned to Chelsea, munching mouthfuls of mushrooms and carrying a bottle of vodka.

It was then things went really weird. The last thing I remember is having mad sex on a pier looking out across the Hudson river as the bats flew above us, and little ships glided past like shooting stars.

Woke up Sunday feeling great.

Iron Lung

Abdullah's been dead three years now. But I saw him last night. I was under the water, being pulled upstream. The water was turquoise-blue; the light of the sun pierced the surface above me. In my left hand, I held a small red paper ball. Abdullah walked along the bank in the opposite direction. He saw the red ball float past and turned back, but I was gone.

What then? I knew that wherever I was it couldn't be a ship – a plane, perhaps, or some kind of spacecraft. I sat on the largest seat on the upper deck. There were no windows. I sat quietly, trying not to be noticed. I didn't have a ticket.

I was a stowaway. But I knew it was my only means of escape.

Abdullah died in a dynamite explosion. The river in my dream was the one that runs along the road from Büyük Cakil to Kas. I am writing this at five thirty in the morning, recalling a dream from the previous night. I haven't slept in more than twenty-four hours.

Is someone looking out for me?

This week I told a friend to burn in hell.

It's now six a.m. and I am smoking. Oh, yeah, Tracey: it's all going so fucking well. The lonely princess. Carbon monoxide is feeding my soul.

'Did you see Tracey?'

'Yes, she was running over Blackfriars Bridge. It was midnight and she was wearing a face mask and carrying a small oxygen tank on her back. Apparently she swims with it.'

'Does she still look beautiful?'

'No. She looked stupid – but she *was* running.'

This week, I swam a mile: sixty-four lengths, the furthest I have swum since 1978. *A Big Day for Tracey*. I tried to tell people about it, but I was drunk: they thought I was talking in riddles or metaphors.

I am changing my body, getting ready for a Caesarean section. I may conceive but my body will never give birth naturally. I want to be unconscious, sunk deep in my own mind, my eyes closed. I want to be as close to death as possible. I want to be cut open like a diamond, my womb raised like a flower, ready to open towards heaven.

That's how I want to bring life into this world. I want my child to greet the world before I look into its eyes.

Why corrupt the innocent with guilt?

In My Dreams

You know that girl you fancy? The one with the dark brown eyes and crooked smile?

Well, I was sitting on her face the other day – my arse pressed right against her nose. I was really drunk, wearing high shoes and staring into the mirror. Her legs were wide open and I was rubbing her clit really fast. I mean *fast* – like I was playing air guitar. She was moaning and whimpering. But me, me, I kept very quiet. I was thinking about that dog, the one that tried to chat me up on the bridge: that small wooden Japanese bridge. It was strange – I mean, no one ever makes a pass at me.

He just stood there, all muscle, wagging his tail. And a

real sexy voice, slow and somehow penetrating. He just came right out with it: 'Trace, do you fancy a fuck?'

I was surprised: first, he knew my name and, second, dogs don't talk. He smiled at me, in a doggy way. 'No,' I told him. I couldn't believe I was talking to a dog.

'What's wrong?' he said. 'Don't you find me attractive?' His face looked kind of hurt and his big eyes seemed to fill with emotion.

'Yeah,' I said. 'You're good-looking, but you're a dog.'

Cocking his head to one side, he looked at me – looked at me like I was shit. 'Tracey, you surprise me,' he said. 'You of all people. I never expected you to be prejudiced.'

By now her black lace knickers were torn to shreds. She was still moaning and groaning.

The cameras were doing a 360-degree spin and the lights were blinding me. His hand was gently rubbing my back. The other was on my hip.

Slowly he pulled me over to the doorway. His hand thrust right up my cunt: a whole fist, like a cork. And behind the fist, enough of my cum to fill a fucking saucepan.

A hood was put over my head and my legs and arms were tied behind my back. I was thrown into the boot of a car.

I woke up to the smell of jasmine and the sound of birds. I was lying on a wooden floor. The phone was ringing. I crawled towards it and knocked the receiver off with my chin.

It was your voice. You said you were coming to save me.

A door opened. You picked me up, threw me on to the bed and started to fuck me like crazy; as though you'd been in prison for seven years, wanking day in day out over panty-liners and support stockings.

My head sank deep into the pillow as though I was losing consciousness – like I didn't exist any more. My soul was in heaven and I was loving you for ever and ever and ever.

And then, I felt the gun. First at my head, the barrel of a shotgun. It was cold, aiming deep into the back of my mind, then – *fuck* – right up deep inside of me. Straight to the neck of my womb.

I was screaming, 'Get it out of me, in the name of God. It hurts. Christ, save me, get it out of me.'

There was blood – blood, deep red blood – everywhere. I was on my back, going crazy, my cunt ripped in two. The cord was cut, I was crying uncontrollably.

My baby was lifted into my arms. You kissed me and I felt beautiful.

Oh God you made
me Feel So beautiful
And Now

I Just want to
Feel it

Again and Again
And Again

New Year in July

I remember, when I was about ten years old, working out that I would be thirty-six in the year 2000. It seemed so far away, so old, so unreal. And here I am, a fucked, crazy, anorexic-alcoholic-childless beautiful woman. I never dreamed it would be like this.

But I will try to ignore the year 2000, as I like to ignore every New Year's Eve.

My New Year's Eve is always 2 July, the night before my birthday. That's the night I make my resolutions. And this year scares the life out of me, because no matter how successful, how good things appear, there is always a deep core of failure within me, although I am trying to deal with it. My biggest fear, this coming year, is that I will be waking up alone.

It makes me wonder how many bodies will be fished out of the Thames, how many decaying corpses will be found in one-room flats.

I'm just being realistic.

Strolling on the plateau of life, desperate for the mountain, I never thought that I would get this far. It's only art that has carried me through, given me faith in my own existence. But now I am approaching a point in my life where I desire more . . .

Over the last few years I have externalised everything, kind of turned myself inside-out. I know that nothing is cut and dried, but I do see two ways to go: either self-preservation, grace and self-respect; or a drunken, decadent orgy of creative lust, pushing myself to the wildest extremes, as far as a person can go without fear. And I don't know which path I will take.

The vainest daydream of all: my funeral. A fleet of black cars travels from London to Margate. It is a beautiful spring day. The light bounces off the cliffs as my thirty-foot funeral pyre is lit. A flock of seagulls circles in the sky. And throughout the night there is a massive party, and even though I am not there, everyone who ever loved or cared about me is . . .

Last year, I made a coffin for myself. It is not coffin-shaped (it always annoys me when I see people dead in coffins, how squashed and tiny they look, no matter how big and charismatic they were in life). It is sky blue, and rather like an ottoman; something I can lie on in comfort, perhaps even have my head propped up, with enough room for my arms to rest gently by my sides. It has a purple mattress, with a hand-embroidered epitaph, fit for an Egyptian queen. I felt very sad during the time I spent making it, and it took months and months. The truth being, of course, that I did not want to finish it: it felt like playing with Fate.

Fuck, I know it's not death I want. It's life, and that really scares the shit out of me. The idea of giving birth. If I was really brave, I would say, 'Yeah, a baby, that's what I want this year.'

I had a dream that I was lying in bed with a man I loved and, between us, this really tiny baby: rose-like face, black spiky hair, wearing a little hand-knitted jumper in Prussian blue.

I told my mum about the dream. She said, 'Tracey, you're not going to have a baby. You can't – you know you can't.'

And I hear myself saying, 'Too fucking right, I can't.' How would it be, the proud mother waking with a hangover from hell? The last thing I'm capable of remembering is vomiting and, somehow, my false teeth going down the toilet and having to fish them out. By this time, it would be three in the afternoon and I would find my body covered with bruises – Christ knows why – with absolutely no memory of coming home. Yet there I would be: brain totally shattered and my skull crushed by an almighty weight.

Aaah. Shit, fuck, hell. No! It would hit me: I'd done it again. Then I'd be phoning round every friend, every bar, and asking the same question: 'Oh, hi, Tracey here. Yes, Tracey Emin.

This is a little embarrassing, but I don't suppose I left my baby at your place last night?'

A mad desire to be more human, to be more normal, that's what pushes me, these days – but as someone said the other day. 'Trace, you're going to have to face facts. You and normal parted a long, long time ago.'

So, my perfect New Year, 2 July. I am floating in the pool at my villa in Cyprus on a bright pink lilo, with a fantastic tan, wearing my Jackie O sunglasses, a shiny black bikini, and drinking a large whisky and Coke, with lots of ice and a slice of lemon. I have a fag in my hand and a big smile across my face. My friends are flying in from all over the world to celebrate my birthday. There are crates of champagne, vodka, whisky and rum; enough of everything to keep us all going for years.

My mobile rings. It is David Bowie: he is coming in on his private jet – *Does anyone need a ride?* The Tate Gallery rings: I've been nominated for the Turner Prize again, and the money's been raised to a hundred grand. I turn down the nomination, not because I'm not interested but because I'm just not in the mood to deal with it. Nick Serota comes on the line to wish me happy birthday anyway.

A fax arrives from Rough Trade records. Pulp's new single, 'Tracey A Girl From Margate' has gone straight into the charts at number one.

Sarah Lucas calls: Virgin Airlines has chartered a special plane to bring everyone over. She says there's been a delay because Mat Collishaw has lost his passport, but he's on his way. They should arrive by six. And my new novel, *Fucked-*

up Crazy Soul, has been banned from all bookshops in the UK. Sarah had been hoping to pick up a copy at the airport.

I put the phone down. And I fall asleep to the sound of helicopters hovering overhead.

I am in a massive double-bed and the clocks are striking twelve. The world may be cheering, but I can't hear. My face is firmly pushed into the pillow and he is fucking me. The year, the time, the date – none of it matters. All I want is him, deep inside me, deeper, for ever and ever.

I'm in love.

The Sun Has Got His Hat On

I got out of the taxi and rang the bell. I had never been into a funeral parlour before but it was exactly what I'd expected: strangely sweet-smelling, sombre music, and a tall, thin man dressed formally in black, speaking in a voice that was far too sincere. Death is a strange thing: there is an overwhelming feeling of powerlessness – full of empty – in knowing that you will never see that person again.

I followed the tall, thin man through a doorway. To my left and right were little rooms, each with a door. Behind each door a body lay resting, waiting. It's a shock when you see someone dead. But the most shocking thing when I looked down at my nan was realising how much she looked like me. And how tiny she was, lying there in pink satin. She was ninety-four years old but in death our faces carried the same bones. She wasn't only my grandmother, she was my best friend: the one I could confide in, the one I would cuddle. We talked about dreams and other worlds. When she couldn't walk any more, I would lie in her bed, and hold her hand while we listened to the radio. And on every visit, I manicured her nails, pedicured her toes, plucked her eyebrows.

I was crying, but when I took a hanky from my bag – a cotton, lavender-coloured hanky – it was to wipe the horrible make-up off her face. They say that when a person dies, their hair and nails keep growing. I took my tweezers and plucked away the unwanted hair from my nan's face. I tried to cut her nails, but her little hands were too tightly clasped together. Instead, I placed a small gift, a note, between the palms.

I had stopped crying. I looked at her and could not believe how beautiful she was, even in death.

I took a photograph of her and sat there in silence. I closed my eyes. Wow, I thought. I'm surrounded by dead people but I'm not afraid. Probably because my nanny's spirit is with me.

Suddenly I heard a loud banging and singing:

'The sun has got his hat on, hip-hip-hip hooray,
The sun has got his hat on and he's coming out today.'

Then the entire funeral parlour was thrown into darkness:

dark, dark, darkness. I fumbled for a light, but if there was a switch anywhere, my hand kept missing it. I couldn't even find the door.

I was trapped in a fucking funeral parlour.

An exit sign made itself visible. I ran towards it and hammered on the doors. I could still hear the singing – it was coming from outside.

Three men opened the door, more scared than I was.

I screamed, 'What the fuck do you think you're doing?'

But I could see what they were doing: they were off on a job, loading a coffin into a hearse. As I walked off into the cold, wintry Margate evening, the last thing I wanted to do was leave my nan there. But maybe she had already gone.

The Mummy Screams

'On the banks of the river . . . der-der-dum' – small hand-clap – 'On the banks of the river Nile.'

I sing in a big black Sudanese, Ottoman-slave-like way. Oh, yes. I am happy. Very, very happy. They say revenge is sweet and it certainly is. I am stretched out on my Sheraton sun-lounger, the west bank of the Nile to the left of me, a circular swimming pool to the right . . .

'Here, I am. Stuck in the middle with you. Stuck in the middle with you. La-la-la.'

I am totally happy. I know it because I keep singing and smiling. I am in the Luxor Sheraton, carried here by night train from Ramses station in central Cairo. Ramses. *Ramses I,*

Ramses II. Good names for a cat: sleek, sexy, cool. For a man, even better. Ram is good, just conjures up the idea of really hard sex.

The last time I was here, four years ago, I swore I would never come back – but I did, determined to eradicate all the memories of that godforsaken cruise. From my sunbed, I can see tourist paddle-steamers like the one that carried me down the Nile last time; ten of them, moored three-deep at the bank. That's no way to visit the Valley of the Kings, chained and manacled to your fellow passengers, bullied and patronised by a resentful tour guide. You need to experience it in your own time. It is the burial ground of ancient monarchs, not a noddy-dog situation, there to be ticked off on a tour list.

We hired our own driver for the day. And the first thing we did when we got into the car was to sack our guide, which takes real assertive action at seven in the morning. Especially through his whimpers of 'But you pay for me.'

'Okay, okay, keep the money. Just get out of the fucking car.'

It was worth paying him off. The tour guides' goal is to get you to the valley by eight a.m., show you three tombs and get you back before you've had time to say, 'Queen Hatshepsut.'

We spent six hours in the valley, avoiding the onslaught of tourists by climbing higher into the hills and visiting the lesser-known kings. Discovering that hidden, internal architecture: serene and minimal, yet built on a vast scale.

I'm not a very good tourist: I'm too much of a snob.

But when it comes to ancient burial sites, I am appalled by the way people lean casually against ancient hiero-glyphs, use flash cameras, make tons of noise. It's worth taking a Walkman just to get rid of the babble of tourist Esperanto . . .

The cruise I took down the Nile, four years ago, was one of the worst experiences of my life. And, no, I wasn't ill: I was stuck on a boat for a week with sixty other people and a really vile tour guide called Naswah. It was hate from the moment we set eyes on each other.

The first thing she said was 'You have no boyfriend, no friends, no parents. Why have you come to Egypt alone?'

In my head, I replied, 'Mind your own fucking business, dog-head.' But, out loud, I think I mumbled, 'I can if I like.'

Oh, God, it was unbearable. The ship was unbearable – the food was gastronomically intolerable. And the people – well, I just drew the short straw. On my table, there was a woman who repeated the end of everybody's sentences, and a bald man who, in the space of a week, grew peculiar egg-shaped lumps all over his head.

I suppose I was the token lone alcoholic with a bad case of Tourette's. After the third day, I could not utter one sentence without using *fuck, cunt, bollocks*, you name it. The waiter would ask if the food was okay – by this point, half of the ship had come down with food poisoning – and I would reply, 'Of course it's not okay. I wouldn't eat this fucking flea-shit if some cunt paid me to.' Which, of course, had a double-whammy effect because the woman who repeated the end of sentences would echo, 'Some cunt paid me to.'

Imagine, sixty people, all bunged up with Immodium, all hating my guts. I was convinced we would soon see Death on the Nile for real.

I jumped ship on a few occasions, to the fury of Naswah. She spent all her time insisting on how dangerous everything was: the bottled water, the cute children selling handmade dolls, drinking tea with the locals, taking *calèche* rides, tipping people. In fact, anything aside from being ripped-off on the boat was considered a mad risk.

I went to Niagara Falls once, at a time when I was very low, feeling as though my life had frozen. I was moving and breathing but everything else had become so slow: I felt that I was trapped inside a still landscape, one of those nightmares where you scream but no one hears. I have always thought that loneliness is the place of fear, where it lives and breathes, where a heavy darkness sets up home in the soul. And while you're engulfed by loneliness, the rest of the world carries on.

It was the depths of winter, and the Falls were tumbling out of an almost frozen world. I wanted to be part of that permanent nature; imagine, to achieve one's goals without question and without doubt, just by being part of that massive flow. I had no desire to jump: I just wanted to die and be a part of it all – the fall of nature.

All very romantic. But have you ever been to Niagara Falls? There is a museum, a quaint little place full of curiosities: fortune-telling machines, strange two-headed animals, the history of the barrel-rollers – they tucked themselves into beer barrels and threw themselves over the Falls. They made every calculation, of course: survival would assure fame and fortune. But most did not survive. In 1880, I might have been one of those people.

In a room upstairs you can gaze at the tortured faces of Egyptian mummies. They have a whole family in the museum: father, mother, children, cats and all. But it is the mother who screams, her mouth wide open, tiny clenched bones. She screams a continuous scream. For herself, as they forced the poison down her throat. For her beloved. And for all the things she loved that would follow her. How can one carry on living without love?

In Egypt, in the Valley of the Kings, there is a tomb. Inside the tomb lies a tiny mummified foetus, curled up small with its big head, hollow eyes and bony little hands. I liked it so much. This *Ramses*, that *Ramses* – I tell you, none of them had anything on this little chap. I wanted to smash my hands through the glass vitrine, hold him in my arms and cuddle him. Dead for thousands of years, not completely formed, but he had soul. He still had soul.

I once made another pilgrimage: to visit Munch's *Scream*. I had spent days crying. My eyes hurt; they were swollen puffy balls. I hadn't eaten or slept properly in weeks and there I was, in Norway, paying homage to my favourite painting. But paying homage wasn't enough, I wanted to jump inside the picture and cradle the Scream in my arms. Another lost soul.

And so I returned to Egypt. A magical place where the

people's honesty can be heart-breaking and the bulrushes really do float past in little basket-shapes. I found a way to visit without fear, exorcising all ghosts from the past to fill my mind with something mind-blowing.

DON'T BE AFRAID TO TAKE THE PAST HEAD ON.

Author's Note

I feel it would be unreasonable for anyone to read a book that had spelling mistakes throughout. It was my decision to have my spelling corrected, and I'm now in the process of learning to spell.